BREAKING UP WITH GOD

BREAKING UP WITH GOD

a love story

SARAH SENTILLES

HarperOne
An Imprint of HarperCollins*Publishers*

HarperCollins books may be purchased for educational, business, or sales promotional use. For information please write: Special Markets Department, HarperCollins Publishers, 10 East 53rd Street, New York, NY 10022.

HarperCollins website: http://www.harpercollins.com

FIRST EDITION

Library of Congress Cataloging-in-Publication Data
Sentilles, Sarah.
Breaking up with God : a love story / Sarah Sentilles. — 1st ed.
p. cm.
ISBN 978-0-06-194686-8
1. Sentilles, Sarah. 2. Spiritual biography. 3. Episcopalians—Biography. I. Title.
BL73.S52A3 2011
283.092—dc22
[B] 2010048656

11 12 13 14 15 RRD(H) 10 9 8 7 6 5 4 3 2 1

For Eric, love.

And for Gordon, gratitude.

LOVE AFTER LOVE

The time will come
when, with elation
you will greet yourself arriving
at your own door, in your own mirror
and each will smile at the other's welcome,

and say, sit here. Eat.
You will love again the stranger who was your self.
Give wine. Give bread. Give back your heart
to itself, to the stranger who has loved you

all your life, whom you ignored
for another, who knows you by heart.
Take down the love letters from the bookshelf,

the photographs, the desperate notes,
peel your own image from the mirror.
Sit. Feast on your life.

—Derek Walcott

CONTENTS

BREAKING UP WITH GOD

PROLOGUE

I BROKE UP WITH GOD. The breakup was devastating. It was like a divorce when all the friends you had as a couple are forced to choose sides and end up not choosing yours. It was like waking up in an empty bed in an empty house. It was like someone I loved died. It was like when Mary Magdalene, Mary the Mother of James, and Salome arrive at Jesus's tomb with spices to anoint his dead body, and they find the stone rolled back, and they look inside the cave, and he's gone.

"God loves you," church signs announce when I drive by. *You shall love the Lord your God with all your heart, and with all your soul, and with all your mind*, Jesus says when he's asked which commandment is the greatest, and in the river, when he's baptized, God claims Jesus as beloved. It's the best love story ever told: God chooses you, sacrifices for you, kills for you, knows you, sees you, saves you. No wonder losing my religion felt like heartbreak.

Still, I hesitate to call what happened to my faith a breakup. I'm not completely comfortable portraying it as a love affair gone wrong. Figuring it as a romance seems simultaneously so medieval-mystic, so patriarchal, so oedipal that it makes me cringe. Even worse, calling it a breakup means I have to come out: I have to admit to myself and to the rest of the world the kind of God I loved—namely, a man. I'm a feminist theologian. Saying out loud that I believed in a male God is like a yoga teacher smoking a pack of cigarettes every day between classes behind the studio. So let's get that part out of the way: I believed in a male God. I loved him. I needed him. Sometimes he was gentle and kind. Sometimes he frightened me.

You could say God and I lived together, which made it hard for me to admit the relationship was over. Staying was easier than looking for a new place to live. God might have been invisible, but he took up a lot of space, and I had never been alone. Sure, the passion had gone out of our relationship, and he wasn't who I thought he was anymore, but we were still comfortable together. Habits, routines, rituals. If you'd gone out to dinner with us, you wouldn't have noticed that anything was wrong, but we definitely didn't run home to tear each other's clothes off. Sometimes we stay with what we know—even if it makes us miserable, even if it makes us feel small—because it's familiar. It's not that misery loves company, it's that we're willing to be miserable if it means we'll have company. I was afraid of being by myself. A dead relationship seemed better than coming home to an empty house.

My relationship with God was never casual. When it began to unravel, I was going through the ordination process to become an Episcopal priest. I was the youth minister at a church in a suburb of Boston and a doctoral student in theology at Harvard. You might say God and I were engaged and the wedding was planned—church reserved, menu chosen, flowers arranged. Calling it off would be awkward.

Breaking up with God meant letting go of someone I had believed in, loved, and built my life around, so I hung on for a long time because I was scared of what would happen if I let go. My relationship with God was connected to everything—my family, my friends, my sense of justice, my vocation, my way of being in the world. I lost more than belief. I couldn't go to the places we used to go anymore. I couldn't use our special language. I couldn't celebrate the same holidays. I even had to trade red wine for beer. People say you can use a simple mathematical formula to figure out how long you will feel like shit after a breakup: one month of pain for every year you were together. God and I were together for my entire life. Thirty-four years. Which translates into thirty-four months of post-breakup misery. Almost three years.

Saying I broke up with God feels like courting divine disaster. The most dangerous time for women in abusive relationships is when they leave. I imagine God browsing the shelves of a local independent bookstore, seeing the title of this book, tracking me down, and smiting me. Doubting is one thing. Actively choosing to end a relationship with God is something else altogether. Not to mention what might happen when God finds out I started seeing other people. He doesn't respond well to restraining orders. He doesn't have a good track record when he's pissed off. He sends locusts, turns women into pillars of salt, kills firstborn children, and drowns people in the sea.

. . .

At the gym a few months ago I saw a woman I know—a friend of a friend of a friend—walking on a treadmill in the last row of exercise machines. She had her treadmill set at a steep angle and was walking quickly uphill. Her headphones were plugged into the television monitor in front of her, and she was watching FOX News.

She took off her headphones and waved me over. She's a teacher, and I'm a teacher, so we chatted briefly about our work in classrooms, and then she said, "I remember you're a writer, but I can't remember what you write about. What are you working on now?"

I considered making something up, telling her I was writing a book about ax murderers or kitchen remodeling, but I told her what I used to tell everyone: "I'm writing a book about losing faith in God."

She hit the red emergency-stop button. "You lost your faith?" she said. Her eyes filled with tears. "I am so sorry. That makes me really sad."

"I'm fine," I said. "Really." I patted her on the arm.

"But I'm not," she said, shaking her head. She gripped the handrail that could count the beats of her heart. "I wasn't born a Christian, but I've been a faithful Christian for twenty-six years. I'm a believer. I've never doubted. Not even once."

I didn't know what to say. I stood there reading the machine's warnings about doctors and dizziness and shortness of breath until she composed her face and smiled. She turned the treadmill back on and walked in place. "You know what?" she said. "We should have dinner sometime." She clapped her hands. "That's what we'll do. We'll get together. We'll drink some wine. We'll talk. Doesn't that sound like fun?"

"Sure. Fun," I said. And then I went directly to the locker room, sat down on a toilet, and cried in the tall square space of the stall. I felt like I did when I dropped out of the ordination process, that it was my doubt that was the problem, not the version of God I was being asked to believe in.

Try a little harder, the faithful say to the doubters. *Ask God to give you strength.*

. . .

In a lecture I heard in college, Ann Ulanov, a professor of psychiatry and religion, compared people of faith to painters, who must remember that a painting of a thing is not the thing itself. She warned we forget the difference between our image of God and God. Our experience doesn't match the image we've created—a child dies, a levee breaks, a job is lost—and the old image of God will not hold. Enraged, we turn from the image and annihilate the first thing we see.

"Much of the violence in the world is misdirected," she said. "We refuse to destroy our images when they don't work anymore." Refuse to unbind canvases, to switch colors, to paint fat over lean. "Turn your violence toward a different target," she said. "Lash out at your images of God. Tear down what you created. Build something new. Believe God can take it."

I made the very mistake Ulanov warned about. I framed God's image in gold. Hung it in my house. Strung up a velvet rope barricade so no one could stand too close or touch it. Armed the alarm. My image of God was God. I thought if I lost my belief, I lost God, and if I lost God, I'd lose everything.

Moses and Aaron and the golden calf, you know the story: Moses goes to the top of Mount Sinai to receive a revelation from God. He's gone a long time. The people he left are afraid. They give their earrings and rings to Aaron. He melts their gold and casts an image of a calf. He builds an altar. People worship. They feast and dance. Moses returns, carrying the tablets, and when he sees the calf and the dancing, when he hears the noise of revelers loud as war, he throws the tablets on the ground, breaking them. He grinds the calf to dust, scatters it on water, and makes the Israelites drink it. Then Moses becomes a horror. He gathers the faithful around him. *Kill your brothers, neighbors, and friends, and atone for what you have done,* he says. Three thousand people are murdered in the desert that day.

At the base of the mountain, even when we think we hear the voice of God, we can never be sure.

Idols are all we ever have.

Maybe the most faithful thing Moses did was smash the tablets.

. . .

My friend Maylen told me a story she heard about a bird trap in India, a platform that turns upside down when a bird lands on it. The upside-down bird believes she'll die if she lets go of the platform, so she clings to it until the hunter comes and carries her away. To escape, all she needs to do is let go. Then she'll fly.

When I knew the God I was with was not the right God for me—that it was over—the voices in my head grew loud and persistent. They seemed to be telling the truth: *You will always be alone. You ruin every good relationship. Your standards are too high. You did something wrong. You will never find anyone to love you.*

In that moment between knowing the relationship must end and doubting you will ever find someone else, you have to believe you are enough. You have to be willing to stand in that empty house and love yourself.

Ending things requires faith.

I

FROM AFAR

No eyes meeting across the room. No first date we never want to end. No friendship that becomes something more. No flowers or gifts or boxes of chocolate or weekend getaways. No funny stories about misunderstandings or missed trains or plans made at the last minute that change everything. No first kiss, no drama, no flutter of butterflies in my stomach, no moment of recognition. It was like an arranged marriage, my faith, God like an older man: He invited my parents to his house. They sipped wine and ate bread. They promised him their firstborn.

If you'd asked me, and if I'd had language, I might have said *water blood cord heart pulse* I might have said *life* I might have said *sleep* I might have said *love* I might have said *darkness* or *milk* or *passage* or *womb* but I would not have said *God*. He was not my first story—but then he became my story, the priest taking me from my parents all dressed in white, the priest marking my head with oil, the priest washing me in water, the priest speaking words like *sin* and *death* and *Satan* and *glamour of evil*, the priest snuffing out the glow of original sin then lighting a candle, the priest wrapping me up, the priest handing me back.

When my mother gave birth to me, there were grape stems in the hospital room under the radiator as if there had been a feast, as if there had been wine, dancing. The doctors gave her drugs during labor, so she forgot she gave birth to me. "Congratulations on your little girl," one of the nurses said.

"I didn't have my baby yet," my mother said. "And I'm having a boy."

My father remembers my beginning differently. "It was cosmic," he says. He knows human beings are made from the explosions of stars, and when he looks at me, this is what he sees. "Stardust," he says, his arm around my shoulders.

My parents bundled me in blankets and took me home to our third-floor apartment in a four-level brownstone in Brooklyn. Our dryer vented out a window in the kitchen, our washing machine hooked up to the bathtub, and sometimes we went to dinner at a Chinese restaurant in our neighborhood, climbed a narrow staircase, ate sizzling rice soup in sticky vinyl booths. After dinner, my father and I sat on the yellow shag rug in our living room and watched *The Muppet Show*, waiting for some animal to blow his trumpet.

. . .

I grew up believing in invisible things.

My sister Emily was born when I was almost three, and we moved to Summit, New Jersey, to a blue house with a big backyard on a busy corner. Elephants lived in our backyard, two of them, a couple. My father named them Mr. and Mrs. Elephantes. Mr. Elephantes's first name was Euphronios, after the ancient Greek potter whose vases were displayed at the Metropolitan Museum of Art, and Mrs. Elephantes's first name was Eustacia. *Eu*, Greek for health and happiness.

We ate dinner at our butcher-block table and looked out the picture window and into the dark and imagined what Mr. and Mrs. Elephantes were doing, how they might be getting along. I pictured them on our swing set, Mr. Elephantes pushing Mrs. Elephantes, feet pumping toward sky, head back.

I watched the elephants and God watched me. And God wasn't just in the yard, but in the sky. In the house. In my room. In my head. My parents and I talked to him every night when they tucked me in: *Now I lay me down to sleep I pray the Lord my soul to keep and if I die before I wake I pray the Lord my soul to take. God bless Mommy and Daddy and Sarah and Emily and Grandma and Grandpa and Grandma and Grandpa and Great Grandma and all the rest of the boys and girls. Help me grow up to be a big, strong, healthy, good girl.* Then kiss goodnight. Then turn out the light. Then darkness. Then solitude. Then God above my bed, somewhere near the ceiling, waiting to take my soul if I died in my sleep, and if I did die in my sleep, a real possibility, it would be because I wasn't the girl God thought I should be. It would be my fault.

. . .

My friends and I thought one of our classmates was a robot. Our proof? Her perfect handwriting that made her homework look like she'd used a typewriter and her white Keds that never got dirty, even at recess. We watched her, waiting for her to make a mistake that would betray her robotic status, but her family moved to California before we could verify she was a machine.

I thought life as a robot would be easier than life as a real girl. I wished I were programmed so I could follow directions perfectly. I wanted to be commanded.

My soccer coach shouted during our games. He'd yell at me to *kick the bloody ball* or to *move up, move up, move up* and I'd try to do exactly what he said. "When your coach yells at you, you just freeze up," my mother said after one game. "You do literally what he tells you to do. It's like you aren't even really playing the game anymore. You stop thinking for yourself."

Sarah, take three giant steps forward.

Mother, may I?

I believed in God the way I played soccer when my coach was yelling at me. It was my responsibility to do exactly what he wanted me to do. Faith was a performance. There was a script.

. . .

My mother didn't want to move to Texas, she didn't want to leave Summit or her friends or her job at the local newspaper, but my father got a new job at a law firm in Dallas where he might make partner. So she packed boxes that were loaded on trucks, and on the day we moved, my parents' friends gathered in our driveway crying in the cold morning darkness. One of my mother's friends accidentally hit me in the ear with her pocketbook. "Don't remember me like this," she said, but that's what I remember most, my ear numb and pulsing.

We drove to Dallas in our stick-shift station wagon with fake wood paneling and no radio. My four-month-old brother screamed for much of the drive, and once my mother held his head out the window.

We arrived in Dallas in May, and my parents convinced administrators at a school named Greenhill to admit me to their first-grade class even though it was almost the end of the academic year.

Holy Trinity was our new church. Before Mass I went to CCD, the Catholic version of Sunday school, and the other students already knew each other, but no one knew my name or bothered to learn it, not even the teachers. We sat in rows and read Bible stories out loud. I asked a lot of questions so I might understand the man I was supposed to love. "It says God hardens Pharaoh's heart. How can God punish Pharaoh for not changing his mind?"

During coffee hour on the stone patio, I asked my father the questions my teachers hadn't answered. He'd gone to Catholic school, he'd been an altar boy and loved to ring the bells at the moment when the bread became body, he'd wanted to be a priest. One Sunday I asked why God would sacrifice His only Son, Jesus Christ—even if it was to save the world—and my father walked me over to talk to one of the priests. "Ask him," he said, holding my hand, but when the priest patiently explained that Jesus went willingly to his death, I didn't feel much better. "Isn't suicide a sin?" I asked.

The priests at Holy Trinity seemed lonely to me. I wanted to know why priests couldn't get married, and my parents told me priests couldn't have their own families because they had to take care of the families in the congregation. "Priests are married to the church," my mother said, and I pictured them in the empty sanctuary on Friday nights, hugging the columns, their voices echoing in all that space. Priests were married to the church, but nuns were married to Jesus, and to me that seemed like the better deal, especially when I saw a painting of a nun lying on her back in bed with Jesus hovering above her. Her arched back made me blush.

Lift up your hearts, the priests said each week in Mass. *We lift them up to the Lord*, we replied, and my head was filled with images of people reaching deep inside themselves to lift up still-beating hearts, blood dripping down their arms and onto their best Sunday clothes. My CCD teacher told me that when God looks down from heaven he sees us all naked and bathed in the blood of Christ. Church was a gory place. It confused me that I had to get so dressed up.

A Sunday School's God

There is one God. And this one God is three. Father, Son, and Holy Ghost. Liquid. Ice. Steam. God's son is Jesus. Jesus's mother is Mary. Mary's husband is Joseph. Jesus suffers and dies on the cross and on the third day he rises from the dead and ascends into heaven and is seated at the right hand of the Father, where he will judge the living and the dead.

God loves you. God loves everyone, but especially the Christians because we're the ones he saved by killing his son, who was Jewish, but not really, because if he had to choose now, he'd be Catholic. *He's got the whole world in his hands. He's got all the little children in his hands.*

God is love, and even though he kills a lot of people in the Bible, he only does it because they deserve it. Jesus didn't deserve it, so God didn't kill him. He sacrificed him, which is different than killing because God did it to make a point—to show us how much he loved us. Or to show us how sinful we are. (I can never seem to remember.)

On Christmas, we celebrate Jesus's birth in the manger because there's no room at the inn and Santa lands his sleigh on the roof and slides down the chimney and brings us presents, and on Easter we celebrate Jesus's death and resurrection and the Easter Bunny brings baskets of chocolate and fake grass and hides pastel-colored hard-boiled eggs for us to find.

God is omniscient, omnipotent, and omnipresent, which means God knows everything, can do anything, and is everywhere at the same time. *You better watch out. You better not cry. You better not pout. I'm telling you why.* God watches you to protect you, but God also watches you to make sure you don't do anything wrong. *He sees you when you're sleeping. He knows when you're awake. He knows if you've been bad or good, so be good for goodness sake.* God knit you in your mother's womb. God counted the hairs on your head. God knows everything about you, even what you're thinking, but that doesn't mean you don't have to pray, because God wants you to say what you're thinking out loud even though he can read your thoughts. It's the saying that matters, although sometimes you can pray without saying anything at all, like after Communion, when you kneel and fold your hands under your chin and try not to let your rear end rest on the pew because you look lazy that way and then God won't answer your prayers.

God loves us so much that he gave us his only son. Then we killed him, but God wanted that to happen, so it's okay. It was all part of the plan. Nothing happens that isn't part of God's plan, and if you ask for something, and God doesn't grant your wish, then it wasn't meant to be, or else you did something wrong and it's a kind of punishment and you didn't deserve whatever it was that you asked for. It's hard to know. *All things bright and beautiful, all creatures great and small, all things wise and wonderful, the Lord God made them all.*

God is invisible, like the wind. God wrote the Bible, but he wrote it through human beings because he can't use a regular pen—well, he could, but it would have to be really big. *Lord, make me an instrument.* Sometimes God tests your faith by asking you to do things that might be unpopular, like asking Abraham to kill Isaac, which means we shouldn't have sex until we're married even if we get pressured at school. *Onward Christian soldiers, marching as to war. Yes Jesus loves me Yes Jesus loves me. If you ever saw him you would even say it glows.*

My mother gave me the gift of suspicion.

She isn't Catholic. She's Episcopalian. She converted to Catholicism when she married my father, and she only attended Catholic Mass to please my father and her mother-in-law. When I asked my mother about the difference between Catholics and Episcopalians, she pointed to the cross. In Catholic churches, she told me, the cross always has Jesus's dead body hanging on it, but in Episcopal churches, the cross is usually empty. "Resurrection," she said.

Catholicism annoyed her. She rolled her eyes during sermons. She rolled her eyes during sappy music. She rolled her eyes at people in the parking lot and yelled, "That's real Christian of you!" when they didn't leave enough room to let us pull out of our parking space.

My mother told me about the parts of the Catholic Church she found problematic—the crucifix, the belief in Limbo, the obsession with the Virgin Mary, the obsession with Latin, the obsession with guilt—and her ongoing critical commentary gave me an early theological education: People tell a lot of stories about God, but only some of them are true.

Sometimes, after Communion, my mother cried, kneeling, her head low, almost touching the shiny dark wood of the pew ahead of us. I asked my father why she was crying, and he told me she missed her mom and dad. They lived in Ohio. When we visited them, we played a game we called The Big Bad Wolf. My grandfather would lie down on his back in the middle of the living room floor, and we'd skip around him in a circle, trying to keep out of his reach singing, *Who's afraid of the big bad wolf, the big bad wolf, the big bad wolf?* until he caught one of us. I screamed when he caught me and tickled me and said he was going to eat my toes. I thought God must be something like that, lying in the middle of the universe with the rest of us circling around him, and I didn't know if I was more afraid that he would catch me or that he wouldn't.

My parents drove us to a French bakery after Mass one Sunday. We stayed in the car and listened to the Top 40 countdown on the radio while they went inside to buy bread for lunch. Chocolate croissant, almond croissant, blueberry muffin, lemon tart, Sacher torte, tiramisu—from glass displays, they chose *palmiers*, layered butter and dough rolled in sugar baked gold. We called them bunny ears and were allowed to eat them on the ride home.

Casey Kasem played Stevie Wonder, and my father turned the dial on the radio to make the music louder. When it was time for the chorus, he turned the dial again, and we all sang, not the words, but the sounds the instruments make between each line Wonder sings.

He sang the first line about calling to say I love you.

"Bing bing," my siblings and I sang.

"Bong," my father sang in his deepest voice.

Then he sang about calling to say he cares.

"Bing bing."

"Bong."

Then Wonder brought it home, singing from the bottom of his heart.

"Bing bing."

"Bong." Casey Kasem and Stevie Wonder, the anticipation of which song would be number one, sweet butter taste of *palmiers,* my siblings close in the back seat of our Suburban, my father's voice—that Sunday refrain on our tongues.

. . .

You will be eating Jesus, the priest said and reminded us what a privilege it was. He gave everyone in my CCD class a shiny gold hardcover book. I wrote my name on the cover carefully in black permanent marker.

The gold book asked me to do things: *make your First Confession*. My mother explained that in the Catholic Church the priest was still the middleman between God and me. I had to tell the priest what I had done wrong so the priest could tell God. "The Protestant Reformation got rid of theology like this," she said. "In the Episcopal Church, we talk to God directly." She didn't understand "what in the world they thought a seven-year-old girl might need to confess," and she promised this would be the only time she'd ever make me go to Confession. I thought about what I would say for weeks.

The day arrived, and I entered where the priest was waiting. We sat in wooden chairs facing each other in that small sunless secret room. My feet didn't reach the ground. I'd never been alone with an adult who wasn't related to me, and I'd never been looked at so directly, as if I had something to say.

I confessed I had been mean to a girl named Sylvia on my soccer team. The other girls and I made fun of her because her clothes were too small and we'd heard she lived in a trailer. The priest told me to say ten Our Fathers and then to ask God for forgiveness. "If you do that," he said, "you will be forgiven." I walked out of the room and knelt in a pew by myself in the dark church and said ten Our Fathers in a row. I asked God to forgive me. I felt something lift. But not everything. Asking God's forgiveness was easy, I thought. Asking Sylvia would be much harder.

The gold book also told me to memorize a prayer: *Lord, I am not worthy to receive you, but only say the word and I shall be healed.* This is what I would say right before Communion, after the priest says, *This is the Lamb of God who takes away the sins of the world. Happy are those who are called to his Supper.* My mother insisted I learn the prayer even though Episcopalians "aren't that into original sin and unworthiness and groveling." She sent me to my room and told me I couldn't come out until I knew the prayer by heart.

I wrote the words again and again, and when I thought I was ready, I walked downstairs, through the dining room, and into the kitchen where my mother was making dinner. *This is the Lamb of God who takes away the sins of the world. Happy are those who are called to his supper,* she said, and the words I was supposed to say disappeared from my mind. She sent me back upstairs.

No matter how many times I wrote the words, no matter how many times I read them out loud, I couldn't memorize that prayer. I didn't want to believe it. I had always believed worthiness was something that belonged to me. I didn't know it had to be granted, earned. I didn't know it could be taken away.

But eventually I did memorize the prayer. It was done.

. . .

All the other girls in my First Communion class wore long white puffy dresses, but my mother refused to dress me up like a miniature bride. "You're not marrying Jesus, for heaven's sake," she said. I wore a short blue and white dress and flowers in my hair.

When I reached the altar, I took the wafer and let Jesus dissolve between my tongue and the roof of my mouth. Then I sipped from the cup. I loved the way Jesus's blood tasted as it evaporated on my tongue, how warm and tingly it made my throat feel when I swallowed it. I was surprised his death tasted so sweet.

After Mass, people came to our house to eat cake, and Aunt Jane, my godmother, gave me a fig tree.

There is a fig tree in Santa Barbara that can shade more than ten thousand people at noon, but my First Communion fig is a tiny thing that still leafs and fruits. My father planted it in the side yard of our house. Its branches stretch out to white brick more than blue sky.

After the promise that she will be like God, that she will not die, Eve eats the fruit from the tree in the garden. She's hungry. She wants to be wise. *We must hide,* she says. *How could we have been naked all this time and not known it?* They sew fig leaves together. They bury themselves in the garden.

Some say the first tamed thing was the fig tree, with flowers that bloom unseen inside its fruit. Only one species of wasp knows about its secret flower, finds the narrow passage, lays eggs, dies. New life hatches, mates. The males, wingless, have a single task: Dig a tunnel for the females' escape. No wonder, then, of all the plants in the garden, Eve chose the fig's lobed leaves to cover her.

. . .

The story of Jesus's baptism—the locust and wild honey–eating, hairshirt-wearing John the Baptist crying out for people to repent, the river, and God descending like a dove. I loved every part of it. When Jesus emerges from the water, a voice says, *This is my Son, the Beloved, with whom I am well pleased.* I watched the sky, waiting for it to open.

I believed God loved me, but his love brought no comfort, just a tightness in the pit in my stomach. God was temperamental, easily angered, unpredictable, suspicious, so I kept my distance. I loved God from afar, like you might love a teacher or a friend's older brother: I watched God carefully and understood everything I heard and saw in church—the liturgy, the stories, the prayers, the music, the artwork, the vestments, the rituals—as a code that when cracked would reveal something important.

I loved God because I wanted God to love me, because I wanted to be worthy. Love was something I did to make him choose me, see me, love me, something I did to keep myself safe. I didn't believe God would love me exactly as I was, just for being me. I thought I had to become the girl God wanted me to be. I acted my part.

I don't call this love now.

. . .

My mother liked just two things about our church in Dallas: Trinity Ministry to the Poor and Father Tom.

Trinity Ministry to the Poor was a food pantry in a small building in the middle of the church's parking lot. The building was beige, temporary, shack-like, shingled, and slant-roofed. It seemed like it should have had wheels like a wheelbarrow. It could be easily lifted away.

People at the church claimed the ministry needed to move because it had outgrown its building, but my mother knew the truth. "They just don't like all those homeless people hanging around," she said. When the ministry was kicked out of the parking lot, we left for a different church, and Trinity Ministry to the Poor relocated to a warehouse downtown. It became a shelter and a place to get job training or to see a doctor. My mother took us there on holidays and in the summers, and we served hot food with ice cream scoops and ladles. We packed brown bags with canned goods. We sorted toys and clothing into piles on the concrete floor. Pam was the woman in charge. My mother said she was a saint.

Father Tom had a beautiful voice. When he sang I thought the roof of the church might open and God might come through. My mother spent time outside the church with Father Tom and a woman named Gladys, both faith healers. Gladys had stigmata.

Stigma, the brand burned on an animal or slave or soldier in ancient Greece. Most stigmatics are women, and most have been starving themselves. Anorexics. Prisoners of war. It's said some stigmata glow in the dark. Some smell like perfume. Doubters—those who think the wounds are self-inflicted—wrap stigmatics' bodies in bandages, lock them in cells, watch all night. *Prove your mind did not do this. Prove your hands did not do this. Prove you did not sharpen stick, pound nail, crack whip, knife skin.*

My birthday is on the feast of St. Francis. The gentle hands of this believer in birds, in wolves, in trees, had the marks of nails in them. They say that on his deathbed, he thanked his donkey for carrying him, and the donkey wept.

I imagined my mother following Father Tom and Gladys from tent to tent. I pictured revival crowds and abandoned crutches, music, speaking in tongues. But I was inventing. Constructing a set. Maybe they met in empty storefronts. Maybe on park benches or in restaurants, darkened booths in the back. I didn't know. My mother didn't tell me. She said only *stigmata*, so I watched my body for signs of God's favor, for love to show itself.

. . .

One of my classmates in third grade, Vanessa, had leukemia. When she felt well enough, she came to school in a wheelchair. She wore a hat because she didn't have much hair. There were lots of stairs at my school, and teachers placed wooden ramps over them so she could come to class. Vanessa missed several weeks of school in a row. They told us she was really sick. I knew I should pray for her, so I did, but only when I thought about her, which wasn't very often.

Our teachers gathered the third graders together. We sat on the rug. *Vanessa died*, they said. All the girls and even a few boys cried. I cried, partly because I felt sad, but mostly because I felt guilty. I could have kept her from dying, but I didn't. I felt God looking at me, disappointed.

After Vanessa died, I asked my mother if Santa really existed. "If you don't believe in him, he won't come," she said. Belief had effects. My mind could betray me. Make bad things happen. I had to control it. I had to believe, or there would be consequences.

I began to pray all the time. My prayers were petitions, but I didn't ask God for clothes or a boyfriend or to help me win a game or do well on a test. I asked God to keep me and the people I loved alive. *Please let us live. Please keep us safe. Please let the plane land safely. Please let the car not crash. Please let no one kidnap me. Please don't make me sick.* I imagined God sitting on a cloud in heaven next to a chalkboard on which all of our names were written, and every time a prayer was said for someone, God put a tally by that person's name.

In my family, death was not natural or inevitable. It could be avoided if you followed the rules. Death happened to other people because they weren't careful enough.

My siblings and I were warned about doing things that could kill us, and I knew if I died while doing them, I would get in trouble. We weren't allowed to swim unless there was an adult outside watching us, and, no, a parent looking through the kitchen window did not count. We weren't allowed to jump on trampolines. We weren't allowed to play soccer if it looked like there might be lightning. During away games, I reminded my coaches that I couldn't play in lightning, and they told me not to worry and to get on the field, and I stood under the darkening sky, looking at the metal bleachers and lights, begging God not to let me die during the game. I always put my seatbelt on immediately when I got in a car, and I never unbuckled even for a second to get something out of my pocket, like lip gloss or gum. I also never sat on anyone's lap in the backseat because I knew what happened if you did that and got in an accident: You flew right out the window, and everyone talked about what a shame it was that you didn't have your seatbelt on because you would have survived the crash if you'd been smart enough to wear one. It was also not a good idea to sit in the back of pickup trucks, to drive a convertible, or to ride in a soft-top Jeep. I imagined my parents at the scene of the accident that kills me, shaking their heads. *We told her not to ride in Jeeps,* they say. *Everyone knows they flip.*

I wouldn't die if I followed the rules. I wouldn't die if I believed.

My youngest sister Della was born when I was in fifth grade. It was Sunday, and my mother took us to church even though she was pregnant and weeks past her due date and my father was at his office working on a deal. Her water broke in the bathroom off the sanctuary. She didn't tell us. She stayed through the end of Mass, drove us home, and sat on the edge of her bed waiting for my father to take her to the hospital. Della was almost born in the backseat of the car. She was blue and didn't have a heartbeat. The doctors revived her and put her in intensive care with all the tiny preemies. My parents gave her the middle name Grace. Her survival, a gift from God, proof of our favor.

. . .

My soccer team, the Gators, played on Saturdays, but I attended a bar or bat mitzvah almost every weekend of seventh grade. After one late-morning soccer game, my friend's mother opened the back of her station wagon, and we took turns climbing into the way-back to kick off our soccer cleats and put our still sweaty bodies into temple-appropriate clothes because there wasn't time to go home and change. She dropped us off at Temple Emanu-El. I stopped to touch the silky yarmulkes piled on a table near the doorway to the synagogue. "Girls don't have to wear those," my friend whispered.

We entered the temple and chose a row of velvet chairs on the right and filed in. I couldn't wait to eat challah. I listened to my classmate chant her Torah portion, thankful I would never have to sing in a foreign language in front of so many people. The rabbi talked about my classmate. He knew the details of her life—her favorite book, what she wanted to be when she grew up, what worried her. That night, he came to the party in a hotel ballroom hours after the ceremony. He wore regular clothes and danced and did the limbo and seemed to enjoy the Michael Jackson impersonator. We broke fluorescent glow sticks in half and painted our lips, our mouths lighting up the dark.

What would it feel like to be Jewish? I memorized the prayer said to bless the wine, *Barukh attah Adonai eloheinu melekh ha-olam, borei peri hagafen*, which means, *Blessed art Thou, Lord our God, King of the universe, Creator of the fruit of the vine.* I knew Jews and Christians believed in the same God, but Jews didn't believe Jesus was the Son of God. I wondered if they felt like they missed something, like the Messiah came, but they didn't recognize him. "What do you think about Jesus?" I asked one of my Jewish friends, trying to seem casually curious and nonjudgmental.

"You know he was a Jew, right?" she said.

. . .

My mother and I went on a retreat in preparation for my confirmation, and it was fun because we spent most of the time sitting in our car hiding from the other kids and their parents. The priest told us to choose a confirmation name. I chose Cecilia because in the illustrated book of saints he passed around St. Cecilia had long blond hair that continued to grow after she died. She looked beautiful in her coffin cushioned by all that yellow hair.

The youth minister made my confirmation class act out the story about the loaves and fishes. Jesus spends the day teaching a crowd of people. It gets late. Everyone's hungry. The disciples tell Jesus to send people away to buy food, but Jesus says, *You give them something to eat.* In their bags they find the five loaves and two fish. Five thousand people sit on the grass. Jesus blesses and breaks and feeds. Twelve baskets of food are left over.

"Do you think Jesus was a skinny little guy?" the minister asked. "Do you think he had a soft voice?" He paced back and forth in front of us, his hands clasped tightly behind his back. "You give them something to eat," he said in a high-pitched, whiny voice to show us that it would have been impossible for Jesus to talk like a woman. "Jesus was big and powerful. He had a booming voice. How else would he get people to pay attention?"

We acted out the story. The boy who played Jesus shouted his lines.

I wish I knew then what I know now: the average height for men when Jesus was alive was 5′1″. He probably weighed 110 pounds. A tiny thing in sandals and a dress.

A Mystic's God

Julian of Norwich loved God so much it made her sick. She stopped eating. They administered last rites. No one thought she'd live. But then she had a vision. She held out her hand, and in it, God placed a tiny round thing the size of a hazelnut. *What can this be?* she asked, and then she heard, *It is all that is made.*

That same year, 1373, Margery Kempe lost her mind after the birth of her first child. She saw devils opening their mouths full of flame. They tried to swallow her. They pawed at her, hauled her around. With her fingernails, she tore her skin. They tied her up. She didn't want to live another day. Then Jesus appeared in her bedroom dressed in purple silk. *Daughter,* he said sitting on the edge of her bed. *Why have you forsaken me, and I never forsook you?* The air in the room opened, bright as lightning. She watched him rise.

Every year my mother gives up wine and saying negative things about other people for Lent. "If it wasn't Lent, I'd say how awful that woman's hair looks," she announces in the middle of restaurants, sipping a margarita.

I gave up dessert in the spring of my sophomore year in high school. "No thank you," I said when people offered me cookies or candy or ice cream. I felt clean, pure, holy, in control, like when the devil tells Jesus after his forty-day desert fast to prove he's the Son of God by eating a stone and Jesus says, *One does not live by bread alone.*

I spent the summer before my junior year at the YMCA down the street from my house. I ran on the treadmill and used the StairMaster and took aerobics classes, jumping around to loud music while our teacher said, "Let's go, ladies. Lift those knees." I measured my thighs to see if my hands could fit around them. I ran my hands up and down my waist and over my stomach to see if it was flat. I ate only yogurt and granola and bran muffins.

When school started again, I made a show of packing my lunch every morning before school—turkey sandwich, bag of chips, green apple, Thin Mints—but I didn't eat lunch at school. I needed to offset all the calories I was sure other people weren't eating because their mothers didn't cook as much as mine did. My mother made big meals every night—pork tenderloin and mashed potatoes and green beans, salad, fresh bread, raspberry pie, and vanilla ice cream.

I thought about food constantly. When I wasn't thinking about food, I was thinking about my thighs and how fat they were. When I wasn't thinking about my thighs and how fat they were, I was planning how to get out of eating dinner with my family. What worked best: telling my mother I wouldn't be home for dinner because I was going out to dinner with a friend. But I didn't eat dinner with my friend. I watched my friend eat dinner, telling her I'd already eaten, and then we ate nonfat frozen yogurt.

I spent hours baking for other people. At school, I gave away caramel brownies and double chocolate cakes and chocolate chip cookies. I tried to burn the rest of the calories I couldn't avoid eating by exercising as much as I could. I was the captain of the field hockey team. I went to practice before anyone else and ran laps around the field and did sit-ups in the grass until my teammates arrived. When I went to the bathroom during school, other girls told me I looked really skinny, maybe too skinny, and I asked if my mother paid them to tell me that.

I felt like everyone was looking at me all the time. I wondered if they could see how disgusting I was. *Lord, I am not worthy to receive you, but only say the word and I shall be healed*. I repeated this prayer in my head, over and over, but I couldn't remember what word to say to be healed. I was so tired, but I didn't let myself eat, and I didn't let myself stop running around and around and around my neighborhood. When it rained, and I couldn't run outside, I ran up and down the stairs in my house. I read magazines full of articles that promised to make me skinnier. One told me to do leg lifts to get rid of saddlebags, which I didn't even know I had until I read about them. I stood naked in front of the full-length mirror in my bedroom. I looked at my image and stared at the pockets of fat. I covered them with my hands to see what my legs looked like without them. I turned sideways to see if my stomach stuck out. I turned around and looked over my shoulder at the back of my body reflected in the mirror. My thighs were enormous.

One night my father and I were about to leave to hear a concert at the museum, but I had to go to the bathroom first. When I came out of the bathroom, my parents were waiting for me in the tiny hallway. "I just need to brush my teeth," I said when I saw them standing there.

"We need to talk," they said. They brought me into their bedroom and closed the door. "We think you have an eating disorder," they said, and I was so relieved I started to cry. I didn't have to keep my secret anymore.

They told me two of my friends called to say they were worried about me. "We watched you and realized they were right," my mother said.

"I'm not who you think I am," I said. I told them I felt like a shell, empty, fake, just doing what people expected me to do. "No one really knows me."

My parents told me they knew me. They told me they loved me the minute I was born, even before I was born, before I had done anything or said anything, and for the first time in my life, I believed them. "Cosmic," my father said, and I knew I was their daughter, their beloved, that with me they were well pleased.

. . .

My therapist, Sidney, asked me to tell her everything I had eaten for the past two weeks, and I did, including the chocolates that I chewed but didn't swallow and spit into the toilet instead. She asked me to buy a notebook and write down everything I ate. I wasn't allowed to skip meals anymore. At the end of our meeting, she gave me a hug, and I wondered if she thought I felt fat. She walked me to the receptionist so I could pay. I walked down the hallway lined with mirrors. I could see cellulite on the back of my thighs.

I drove to a nondescript, tan building on the side of a highway every week to talk with Sidney. I tried to arrive early so I could read magazines in the waiting room. I studied the celebrities and models who made being thin look effortless. I couldn't turn the pages fast enough. I wanted to know everything—what they ate, how they exercised, what their relationships were like. When Sidney came to get me from the waiting room, I closed whatever magazine I'd been reading and felt sick to my stomach, as if I had just eaten too much candy.

Each week Sidney made me tell her a part of my body that I liked and was thankful for. "I like my eyelashes," I said.

"Good," she said.

The next week I told her I liked my wrists.

The week after that, fingernails.

"You're going to run out of things like that," she said. "Try to find a bigger part of your body to love."

Sidney wouldn't diagnose me because she didn't think a diagnosis would help me heal. I thought I was anorexic, but my parents thought I was bulimic, and I thought that meant they thought I was too fat to be anorexic. My mother kept accusing me of throwing up because I went to the bathroom after every meal and then brushed my teeth. I could see she was frustrated with me, tired of me not eating the meals she prepared, annoyed I was always a special case. She tried to show me that my behavior was irrational. "If you really want to lose weight so badly, why do you eat so much granola?" she asked. "You should probably eat something less fattening."

Sidney asked, "What do you want your body to look like?"

"I don't know," I said. "Skinnier than this."

"If you don't know what you want to look like, how will you know when you're done?"

I heard her question and knew I would never be done. A lifetime of dieting and running in circles stretched out before me. I was not just trying to get skinnier. I was trying to be smaller, to take up less space. I was trying to become someone else, someone worthy. Whoever I was, was not who I wanted to be.

I wouldn't be allowed to go to college if my parents thought my life was at risk, but we spent the fall of my senior year working on college applications anyway. My mother and I went on an East Coast college tour. We flew in a plane and rented a car and drove from college to college, my mother drilling me with practice interview questions. "What's your favorite class?" she asked.

"I'm not sure," I said. "I guess I like them all."

"That's not a good answer," she said. "Make something up if you can't decide. They'll want to know you have opinions, that you're decisive."

We were standing in Harvard Yard, surrounded by the dorms where the freshmen live, and I needed to go to the bathroom. It was an emergency. "The dorms are off limits for the tour," our guide said.

"But I really need to use the restroom," I said.

The guide opened the door to one of the entryways and let me in. "If she gets to see the dorms, my daughter gets to see the dorms," one of the parents in our tour group said looking around at all the other parents in the group. "It's only fair."

I applied early to Yale, and in December I was accepted. I applied to a special poetry program for freshmen, and I got into that, too. Sidney told my parents they needed to let me go, that I was ready for college, that I was recovering. They believed her.

. . .

The hemorrhaging woman has been bleeding for twelve years. No one has been able to help her. She is one person in a huge crowd asking Jesus to heal them. She touches the fringe of his clothes and stops bleeding. *Who touched me?* Jesus asks. The woman comes forward, trembling. She falls down at his feet. *Daughter, your faith has made you well,* Jesus says. *Go in peace.*

A man named Jairus is there, too. He begs Jesus to come to his house to heal his only daughter. She is twelve, and she is dying. Someone comes from Jairus's house to tell him his daughter has died. *Your daughter is dead*, he says. *Do not trouble the teacher any longer.* But Jesus says, *Do not fear. Only believe.*

They go to Jairus's house, and when they enter the house, everyone is weeping, wailing. Jesus says, *Do not weep; for she is not dead but sleeping.*

They laugh at him. They know she is dead.

Jesus takes Jairus's daughter by the hand. *Little girl, get up!* he says, and she gets up at once. Then Jesus says, *Give her something to eat.*

. . .

Sidney's office was a small, windowless room, but when I was in it, I felt the world expand. I let myself take up space. During our last session together before I left for college, Sidney told me I was good. She told me I was beautiful. She told me I was ready to be free.

Little girl, I heard, *Get up*, and then, *Give her something to eat.*

2

THE ART OF LOVE

I WENT TO CHURCH in Dallas because I didn't want to die. I went to church to keep God from punishing me. It was like knocking on wood, like throwing salt over my shoulder. I wondered if God really kept track of who went to church and who didn't. This version of God seemed small to me, like the priests shrunk him to make him fit in the building, but I was too superstitious, too afraid, not to go to church.

I also went to church because my parents made me go, but there was no one to make me go to church at Yale, and organized religion suddenly felt like virginity—something better left behind. I treated God like some of my classmates treated their boyfriends or girlfriends who were still in high school: I hid him. I didn't put up any pictures of him. I talked about him only in the most general terms, using words like "religion" or "spirituality" or "meaning." In public, my relationship with God became abstract, theoretical. I spoke about it in the past tense. "I grew up Catholic," I'd say when religion came up in conversation. "Me, too," the other person would say, and we'd roll our eyes.

But late at night, when no one else could hear me, I talked to God for hours. I was afraid something bad would happen to my family while I was away, and I begged God to keep them safe. What at first I did only at night soon became a habit, a chant, an incantation that ran over and over in my head, all the time, when I was walking to class, reading in the library, eating meals in the dining hall. *Please keep them safe. Please keep them safe. Please keep them safe.*

I wasn't the only one who stopped going to Mass when I went to college. My mother left the Catholic Church completely. She announced that she'd given the Catholics twenty years, and the rest of us "could do whatever we wanted," but she was returning to the Episcopal Church. "I'm going home," she said. "I need to be someplace where God can hear me and I can hear God."

The rest of my family followed her, and my Catholic grandmother was devastated because she knew we were going to hell. When I visited her over that first Thanksgiving break, I sat on the white carpet in front of the blue chair where she said the rosary and made needlepoint Christmas ornaments. She rubbed my back gently. "Don't worry, Sarah," she said. "I promise I'll wave to you from heaven."

. . .

The dean of my residential college played a joke on all the freshmen and filled our suites on Old Campus with people who had the same first names. There were suites of Toms and Lauras and Johns. There was a suite of Sarahs, too, although I wasn't assigned to it. I climbed the three flights of stairs to my room and met three Jennifers. When our dorm phone rang and people asked to speak with Jennifer, we had to ask, "Which one?" and because it was the first year of college, and no one knew anyone's last name, the person on the other end of the phone never knew what to say. Some callers described their Jennifer. "She has long blond hair," they said, which didn't help because all the Jennifers had long blond hair.

One night in the middle of the year, one of the Jennifers tried to commit suicide in the room next to mine. She was a poet and she was in love, but her parents wanted her to be a doctor and break up with her boyfriend.

I heard her crying through the wall we shared, and then her room was silent. One of the other Jennifers knocked on her door, "Jennifer? Jennifer? Are you all right?" She didn't answer. We pounded on her door with our fists and shouted her name. We called 911, and an ambulance arrived, and our freshman counselor unlocked her room for the paramedics, and I saw Jennifer lying on her bed, asleep, an empty bottle of Tylenol next to her.

The doctors pumped her stomach and sent her to the mental health unit at Yale–New Haven. We visited her there. Heavy locked doors, thick glass, skeletal women in wheelchairs everywhere. "I'm with all the eating disorder patients," Jennifer said, and I looked at the pale, starving women not strong enough to bear their own weight, and I felt relieved and ashamed, and on our walk back to the dorms I touched my stomach and felt fat.

. . .

I wore linen Bermuda shorts covered in peach flowers, a matching peach T-shirt, and a white linen jacket on my first day at Yale. I went outside to meet my new classmates, and most of them were wearing baseball caps and jeans and T-shirts that said Exeter or Andover or St. Paul's or Choate or Groton. I hadn't gone to boarding school. I didn't own a single pair of jeans. I needed help. "Is this casual?" I'd ask my roommates every morning, and they'd look at my outfit and tell me to take off my belt or untuck my shirt, and one day they suggested that maybe it was time to stop hot-rolling my hair. To make our lives easier, I decided to wear black—black jeans, black shirt, black cowboy boots, every day. The only nonblack thing I still wore was the hot pink and red Native American print winter jacket my mother and I bought in Dallas that looked warm but was made out of cotton. I spent most of my freshman year freezing.

Soon after I stopped going to church, but before I dressed in black, I fell in love with a Canadian with shaggy brown hair long enough to tuck behind his ears. Canada told stories that made everyone laugh. I was surprised when he called my room to see if I'd like to hang out. He was the coolest boy who'd ever paid attention to me, and it felt like an accident, like he made a mistake when he chose me, but he kept calling and playing Led Zeppelin songs on his guitar. We spent all our time together when we weren't in class, meeting between classes in hallways or on street corners. At first I rushed to meet him because I couldn't wait to see him. Then I rushed to meet him because he was mad and suspicious when I was late. His room overlooked a busy corner on campus, and I felt him watching me when I passed under his window. I looked up but could never see his face through the glass.

Before I left for college, my mother took me to a department store to buy a green comforter—"It will match your eyes," she said. She also took me to a doctor to get birth control pills. My mother, the doctor, and I pretended I needed the pill because my periods were irregular, but we all knew I needed the pill so I wouldn't get pregnant as soon as I stepped foot on a college campus. Birth control was something my mother had always supported, even when she was Catholic. "The pope has no idea what he is talking about," my mother said. "How could he? He's not even allowed to date."

I hadn't yet had sex when I arrived at Yale, but if Catholicism taught me anything, it was that virginity would not necessarily protect me from pregnancy. Mary, the Mother of God, was a virgin, and she got pregnant. I imagined what I'd say if it ever happened to me. "No, really," I'd say, calmly rubbing my growing belly. "I'm a virgin and an angel told me I'm going to have God's baby."

People talked about virginity like it was an object, a family heirloom, or an expensive piece of jewelry you had to keep track of and insure because once it was lost you couldn't replace it. I was afraid to lose mine, but virginity also felt like a setup—something invented to get women to behave—and I wanted to be done with it. It was too heavy to keep carrying around.

I decided to have sex with Canada. "I'm ready," I said one night while we were making out and rolling around on my bed, and the whole thing was over before I even knew it had started. *That's it?* I thought. *I waited all this time for* that?

. . .

I tried out for the field hockey team my sophomore year and made the team. During an away game, I broke my middle finger. It was sleeting, and I was playing defense. On a short corner, I rushed out of the box toward the ball, and the forward from the other team swung her stick hard, and my finger got caught between her stick and my own. Because it was so cold, I didn't notice my finger was broken until I looked down and saw that the first joint of my middle finger was at a right angle. "My hand really hurts," I said to the referee. "All our hands hurt," she said. "It's freezing out here."

I showed her my crooked finger, and she blew her whistle to stop the game. The trainer packed my hand in ice for the two-hour bus ride home. My coach drove me to the emergency room when we were back in New Haven. I called Canada and told him where I was. He had a car and said he would drive to the hospital to be with me. I was ushered into the examination room before he arrived. The doctor told me they would have to re-break my finger because it had already begun to set. He told me I needed surgery and that doctors would put two pins in my finger. I was with the doctor for a long time, and when he let me go, I walked through the waiting room and didn't see Canada. I figured he got tired and went home because it was almost two o'clock in the morning. I had no way to get in touch with him, so I took the shuttle back to my dorm room.

My roommates were waiting for me. They made me a toasted cheese sandwich in our toaster oven. I took two bites of the sandwich before Canada stormed into the room. "I waited for you all night!" he said. "And you left without me!" I put down my sandwich and brought him to my bedroom. I tried to calm him down, but he was furious. He yelled. He grabbed my shoulders and put his face close to mine. He shook me, and then he left. I went back to our common room where my roommates were. I picked up my cold sandwich and took a bite.

"We heard him yelling at you, Sarah," my roommates said. "He wasn't yelling at me," I said and tried to laugh it off. "He was just worried about me because he didn't know where I was."

That was the first time Canada shook me, but it wasn't the last. He would shake me again, and grab my leg, and grab my arm, and call me a bitch and a slut and tell me I must have been lying when I told him I was a virgin when we met because I liked sex too much for him to have been my first. But I didn't break up with him, not even when he cheated on me. Canada broke up with me, and I was inconsolable. I still rushed to the places we used to meet after class, but he was never there. I spent hours in my room playing Annie Lennox's "Why" over and over and over again until my roommate told me she loved me, and she knew I was upset, but if I played that song one more time she would throw the CD out the window.

I tried so hard to be the person I thought Canada wanted me to be that without him to mold myself to, I had no shape. When he broke up with me, I shouted, "You don't even know who I am," but I was talking to myself: I didn't know who I was. I felt small and defenseless and broken, and part of me liked feeling that way because it was familiar and no one expected much from hurt little things. I imagined myself like a bird pushed out of the nest too soon. I joked about it with my roommates, folding my arms like wings and awkwardly flapping them saying, "wounded bird, wounded bird."

. . .

In "The Poems of Our Climate" Wallace Stevens describes a bowl filled with clear water and pink and white carnations in a room with light "like snowy air, / reflecting snow." "What can you see in that clear water?" my poetry seminar professor asked.

"Everything?" I said.

"No," she said. "Nothing. It seems to show you everything, but it's transparent. We see through it. We see whatever is around it."

I was like that bowl of clear water. I seemed to show everyone everything about me, to hide nothing, but you could see right through me. I was all artifice. I was whoever you wanted me to be.

After we moved to Dallas, when I was in second grade, I had a friend over to play, and after a few hours, my friend's mother came to pick her up. My mother stood at the front door and told my friend's mother how much we enjoyed having her daughter at our house. When they left, my mother closed the door and looked at me. "You turn into whoever is around you. You're such a chameleon," she said. "Where does my Sarah go?"

After the class on Stevens, I walked back to my room repeating the last three lines of his poem:

Note that, in this bitterness, delight,
Since the imperfect is so hot in us,
Lies in flawed words and stubborn sounds.

I had to speak slowly. The words caught on the tip of my tongue. I imagined the imperfect inside me, bubbling up, spilling out like lava, and I remembered the pumice stone I held in Hawaii during a family vacation and how surprised I was that lava could become so light.

. . .

I decided to major in literature because I love to read. My black clothes helped me fit in at the smoke-filled Daily Café, where all the literature majors hung out and drank coffee and talked about Jacques Derrida.

The literature department was dominated by deconstruction. My professors taught me that the word "tree" was not the same as the tree itself. The word "book" was not the same as the book itself. Everything could just as easily be called by another name. Meaning was unhitched, unmoored, destabilized. Truth is not something we discover, not something we find, my professors told us. It is something we make.

Some of the theorists we read argued that exposing truth as a construction made everything meaningless. We can never say what we mean to say, they wrote, and even if we could, no one could understand us. Other theorists reveled in truth's status as construction. There is a surplus of meaning, they argued, not an absence of it. For them, the space between the word and the thing left room—for art, poetry, transcendence.

I was still praying to God all the time, still hoping that if I prayed often enough and hard enough no one I loved would die. But as I sat in those classrooms, a different version of God began to take shape in my mind—the God from Genesis, the poet and the sculptor who uses words and clay to create the world. "Let there be light," God says, and there is light. "Let dry land appear," God says, and dry land appears. "Let the birds fly above the earth," God says, and the birds fly above the earth. God forms humans out of mud and breathes into them. And they sit around a table drinking coffee thousands of years later, talking about it.

I felt my childhood version of God starting to disappear. Make-believe, I thought. It's all make-believe. We make, and then we believe.

. . .

I took a tour of Yale's buildings led by an art historian, and we walked from building to building while our guide pointed out all the artwork that depicted women—stained glass images of women in flowing dresses, statues of women personifying wisdom, paintings of women symbolizing the *alma mater.* "These images were made when women weren't allowed to go to school here," she said. "What does it mean to build a university that is only for men and to fill it with images of women?"

I remembered a set of stone steps I'd heard about. In the middle of a city, the steps were built to match a woman's stride. If someone—a mugger, a rapist—were chasing a woman, she would be able to run up the steps more quickly than her pursuer. She would be able to escape.

How did they determine the length of a woman's stride? Did they ask a woman to run? Did they say, *Imagine someone is chasing you*?

Maya Lin built a memorial to honor women at Yale. A fountain, an oblong stone, dark and flat, water flowing from an off-center hole and spilling over the edge. "It's not phallic. It's yonic," one of my friends said, and we laughed, repeating the word that meant the fountain was like a vagina. Etched onto the stone is a spiral of numbers, one number for each year Yale has been in existence. Next to each year is the number of women who were students at Yale during that year. There are a lot of zeros.

In my Virginia Woolf seminar, we were only allowed to use pencil when we underlined or wrote in the margins of Woolf's books. "Would you write on someone's painting?" my professor asked. "This is her art, and your notes are only your thoughts about her art." She told us Woolf didn't want any human figures on the covers of her books. "But look what the publisher has done!" she said, holding up her copy of *To the Lighthouse* with a painting of a woman looking out a window on its cover. I checked out commentaries on Woolf from the library and recognized my professor's handwriting in the margins. *No*, she penciled on the book's pages in tiny tight cursive. *No, no, no*!

In *To the Lighthouse*, Lily Briscoe, a painter, struggles to put her vision on canvas: "She could see it all so clearly, so commandingly, when she looked: it was when she took her brush in her hand that the whole thing changed. It was in that moment's flight between the picture and her canvas that the demons set on her who often brought her to the verge of tears and made this passage from conception to work as dreadful as any down a dark passage for a child. Such she often felt herself—struggling against terrific odds to maintain her courage; to say: 'But this is what I see; this is what I see.' "

It was the beginning of World War II, and Woolf was afraid she was going mad again. She had lived through the first World War and couldn't live through another day of bombs falling on her city. Not one more day. She left two notes, one to her husband, Leonard, and one to her sister Vanessa. To Leonard she wrote, *If anybody could have saved me it would have been you.*

Reading about Woolf's suicide and the stones she put in her pocket and the river she walked into frightened me. Words did not save her, would not save human beings from war or from each other. All that mattered was the weight of stones. I pinned a black-and-white photograph of Virginia Woolf to my dorm room wall.

When I started going to therapy in high school, my mother was already seeing a therapist in the office next door to Sidney's. I asked her why she was seeing a therapist, and she said her anger scared her. "One morning I went out to get the newspaper from the front lawn, and I thought, maybe I should just keep walking and never come back."

. . .

Woolf writes that even Jane Austen didn't have a room of her own. She wrote in a sitting room and was always interrupted. My mother writes in a room smaller than a closet, just off the living room. Before it was her office, it was a wet bar with an ice-maker and cabinets full of glasses and liquor. My mother never closed the door, and when we were children, we talked to her constantly. "Can you please give me five minutes?" she asked. "Just five minutes?"

My parents met on a blind date at the end of their senior year in college. When they graduated, my mother went to journalism school, and my father went to law school. They lived in different cities, but they continued to date each other. When my mother finished her master's degree, she got a job in a newsroom in Ohio. She was the first female broadcaster on television there. "I couldn't believe I was getting paid to do something I loved so much," she said.

My father asked my mother in an airport parking lot to marry him. He had split his lip playing tennis and got the stitches taken out so he could propose. "Right here?" she asked. She left her job and Ohio so she could move to New Haven to be with my father while he finished law school. She didn't get another job as a reporter. She worked as a bank teller. Then my father was hired by a law firm in New York City, and they moved to the apartment in Brooklyn. I was born. Emily was born. We moved to Summit. Irwin was born. My mother wrote a regular column in the town's newspaper, but then we moved to Dallas, and she had to leave that job, too. Then Della was born. My mother became a ghostwriter, writing speeches and articles and essays other people put their names on.

While I was in college, a documentary about my mother's class at Wellesley—the class of 1969, Hillary Clinton's class—aired on PBS. My mother sent me a copy, and I watched it with my roommates sitting on the floor of our common room. Several women are interviewed in the film. One sacrifices everything for career. One tries to balance work and family. And one—my mother—sacrifices everything for family.

They show old footage of her as a television reporter in Ohio. It was as if I'd never seen her before.

. . .

I didn't drink in high school, and I didn't drink until Canada and I broke up. Although Canada drank, he liked that I didn't. "You're pure," he'd say. "You're my Texas rose." I didn't know what it meant to be a Texas rose, but I liked having a boyfriend because it was a reason not to go to any parties, which meant I didn't have to drink or justify why I wasn't drinking. "I'm meeting Canada later," I'd say when my roommates left to go out, and I would stay in my room and read.

Now that we weren't together anymore, I had no excuse. I didn't go to any parties in high school. I was afraid I wouldn't know what to do when I got there, and I couldn't stop picturing the police my mother told me would arrive wielding giant flashlights and handcuffs to round us up and take us to jail. My roommates dragged me to a few parties, and I stood around awkwardly with nothing in my hands. One Saturday night we walked up Science Hill to an off-campus apartment, and I talked to a guy I had a crush on. I didn't know what to say standing next to him, so I looked around and saw an umbrella holder next to the front door. "I've always wanted an umbrella holder," I said.

I visited a friend at a nearby college at the end of my sophomore year, and she took me to a party full of people we went to high school with. Their delight at seeing me at a party intoxicated me before I took my first drink. We toasted each other with Bellinis, sweet as peach Jolly Ranchers. After Bellinis, Goldschläger—thick cinnamon liqueur flecked with real gold—and after Goldschläger, beer out of clear plastic cups in the basement of an eating club. Before I knew it, I was on the floor next to a toilet throwing up.

Bellinis are named after the color of a saint's toga in a painting by the Italian Renaissance artist Giovanni Bellini. In a different painting by Bellini, *Transfiguration*, Jesus stands on the flat top of Mount Tabor, Elijah on one side, Moses on the other. The story says that Jesus's clothes glow white, so bright they blind Peter, James, and John. But in the painting, the disciples look asleep, as if they were so tired they spent the night wherever they fell.

. . .

My roommates and I ate dinner at our friends' off-campus apartment every Thursday night. A man with a pet snake lived in their building, and he wandered around carrying his snake and made the place feel like Eden. We ate lasagna and bread and drank red wine late into the night. One Thursday, we talked about my mother's documentary on PBS, about the women and the choices they made. We felt sorry for them, convinced we would be able to do it all, to have it all. Love. Children. Careers. "People say you can't have your cake and eat it, too," my friend Maylen said. "But that doesn't make any sense. It isn't your cake if you can't eat it."

Someone handed me a baguette, and I ripped off a piece of bread. I wanted to say, *This is my body. Take. Eat,* but I knew that would be too melodramatic. "This is so fun," I said instead, and my friends laughed because I couldn't let the moment be.

I still name the fun I'm having because it always surprises me. The abandon. The absence of tightness in the pit in my stomach. The feeling of connection. The joy. It's as if I think by saying *This is fun* I can make the good feelings stay, keep the other shoe from dropping, but my words betray my fear of ambush, the shame sitting in the corner of the room. *Who do you think you are?*

When summer came, we took a ferry to Block Island and walked to a rocky beach and put stones in our mouths, tasting salt and sunlight and sea. We sat on the beach or in weathered Adirondack chairs or around a table in the kitchen. There was a thunderstorm one night during dinner, and lightning hit the house. It sounded like something splitting open. The lights went out. We lit candles. I remembered a sign my grandfather had in his workshop: *Watch for Lightening.* My grandfather hung the sign because he thought the spelling error was funny, but at that table with my friends, I thought the sign maker had not made a mistake at all.

. . .

I took the Phenomenology of Religion my senior year, and our narrow classroom was packed with students. When Louis Dupré spoke the class was silent. A small Catholic man with bright white hair, he seemed to glow, to float. Words fall short because they must, Dupré said. This is not failure. This is possibility. I thought if Virginia Woolf were in that class, Dupré could have kept her from walking into the river.

Imagine you are looking at a painting of a landscape, he said. You know it is a painting, that it is just paint brushed on a flat canvas, but when you look at the painting, another world opens in front of you, so much so that you turn over the canvas to see what is on the other side and are surprised when all you find is blank canvas stretched over wood. Religious symbols open like that painting. Religious language is odd language. We use it to describe an extraordinary situation in ordinary words; we use ordinary words to disconcert normal expectations.

Think of Moses, Dupré said. Look how ordinary everything is in his story. A flock of sheep, wilderness, a mountain, voices, a bush, flame, sandals, bare feet. But the bush is not consumed. And the voice does not belong to a body. And the name God gives is no name at all: "I AM WHO I AM." God tells Moses his name is being.

What does it mean to say that God is being itself? Dupré asked. Then he answered his question with a love story: Imagine you fall in love, he said. Your love will start innocuously. You will fall in love with the other's eyes, with the other's hair and lips. But if your love is serious, it will not be about features. It will be about what remains when all that beauty is gone, when all that is left is bareness. That is Being. The most intimate part of yourself. That is God. He paused, and the classroom filled up with silence. We waited for him to speak again. I found what he said in my notebook: In that intimate space, God and I touch, and we are truly divine.

"Holy shit!" we said to each other as we filed out of Dupré's classroom to a bar called Rudy's. I played bar basketball and won free beers from men who thought they could beat me but couldn't. Then we went to Toad's and danced to "Here Comes the Hotstepper" and then to "I Will Survive," which seemed, somehow, to be about transcendence now. We kept talking about Dupré and the place where the divine and the human touch, while we watched people grind on dance floors and stand on rooftops of fraternity houses wearing capes. We used long plastic straws to drink alcohol out of big bowls and walked home drunk, stumbling and laughing and stopping to pee between buildings. We went to the convenience store down the street called WaWa for SunChips and Snackwells, and we watched hot dogs roll around under heat lamps while we stood in line to pay, wondering who ordered hot dogs at a convenience store.

. . .

Dupré told us about Isaac Luria, a fifteenth-century Jewish mystic who believed when God created the world, he made an emptiness in himself. He made a place for otherness. He made himself vulnerable and weak. The creative act is an expression of a fundamental uncertainty. It changes God. It makes a hole in God.

I need God for all I am, Dupré said. And God needs me for all God is. God needs me to be God. God is the life force of everything that is, he said. God is everywhere, the core of everything that is. Most Christians and Jews are too afraid of pantheism to admit this, he said. Mystics are not afraid of pantheism. They know if God is not in the movement of my fingers, then God does not exist.

I speak to you as an older person, Dupré said. Life is a series of failures, and at the end, you die, no matter how successful you are. This life is flawed and fragile, and we are vulnerable. Life is no more than that. But religion says that the meaning of life is not in your narrow way of looking. Religion tells us we have infinite capacity.

Religion is this: the one thing able to tell you that you have any significance at all.

Dupré showed us the painting of Adam and God, you know the one, all clouds and outstretched arms and wind. I don't like this painting, Dupré said. I don't like that their hands aren't touching. Imagine there is no space between their fingers. That would be a more accurate way to tell the story. There will always be a point where they meet, he said, because anything created by God is God. Adam's fingers are never released.

3

GOD + SARAH = LOVE

I APPLIED TO Teach for America because I wanted to do something that mattered and because I wanted to have an answer that would make me appear brave and generous when people asked what I was going to do when I graduated, a display of civic responsibility. *Are you there, God? It's me, Sarah, doer of good deeds.* I had worked at a middle school in Harlem the summer before my senior year, so I asked the director of that program to write a letter of recommendation for me as part of my TFA application. She said no. Teach for America, she told me, undermines teaching as a profession and turns what should be a right—access to an excellent education—into a charity project, sending do-good, well-intentioned, untrained teachers into classrooms that need the best, most well-trained teachers, and then they have the gall to say, *Aren't those children lucky? Their teacher went to Yale!* I ignored her and convinced three professors to write letters of recommendation for me. I applied and was accepted, assigned to the Los Angeles corps, where I'd be teaching elementary school for two years in Compton, a city in south central Los Angeles.

At a five-week training institute in Houston for all TFA corps members, I designed lesson plans for imaginary students. I turned my plans in, and they were returned to me, graded, with few comments. One of my new friends put a recipe for guacamole in the middle of his lesson plans because he didn't think anyone was reading the plans closely, and he got an "A."

In groups of four, we taught summer school classes in Houston's public schools. My group's mentor was twenty-two years old and had been a kindergarten teacher for just six months. Before that, she'd been a cheerleader. She made us practice phonics routines every morning until the students arrived. We sat on the carpet with her standing in front of us and clapping her hands loudly and shouting, "Give me an 'A!' "

"Ah ah ah ah ah," we chanted.

"Give me a 'B!' "

"Buh buh buh buh buh."

"We are so screwed," one of the people in my group whispered.

She held a brown teddy bear in front of her. "Do you see this bear?" she asked. "This is Officer Bear." It works like this: Put Officer Bear at the front of your classroom in a chair next to a telephone, tell your students Officer Bear can see everything they do and hear everything they say, and if they're bad, Officer Bear will call the police, and the police will arrest their parents and take them to jail.

We prepared a unit for kindergarteners based on shapes, but when our six students arrived for summer school, they could identify triangles and squares and rectangles, but they didn't know how to draw them, so none of our lessons made any sense.

I attended TFA classes at night about calendar math and bulletin boards and reward systems. I couldn't wait to have my own classroom—to decorate, to make rules, to be in charge. My savior complex.

Some of us stayed up late to talk about race. "I'm worried that people in Compton will make judgments about me because I'm white," I said.

"Welcome to my world," an African-American woman said.

. . .

Soon I was spending most of my time with another corps member from Texas. He lived in Austin and, like me, would be moving to Los Angeles. I told him I had a crush on him and Austin told me he had a crush on me, too, but he also told me he had a girlfriend, so whatever happened between us couldn't be too serious. "Let's just keep things casual," he said.

"Sure," I said. "Let's keep it casual," but I knew we were meant for each other. He *got* me. He listened. He let me show him all of my pictures from college. We did word puzzles together. And even though he kept telling me he needed to keep things casual because he had a girlfriend, I knew he really meant to say, *I'm falling in love with you, but it scares me*, so I had sex with him in the back of my car because we were living in dorms at the University of Houston and there was nowhere else to go.

TFA posted a handwritten list of names that included Austin's on the wall of the cafeteria. He'd been reassigned and would be staying in Houston instead of moving to Los Angeles. We kept having sex in the back of my car, and everything felt desperate and beautiful, like each time might be the last.

At the end of the summer institute I went on vacation with my family, and when I returned, I made the four-hour drive from Dallas to Houston to see Austin in his new apartment before I moved to Los Angeles, even though he hadn't called me once while I was away. He went to play basketball with his friends when I arrived and left me sitting on his couch. His phone rang, I answered it, and it was his girlfriend. When he got back from basketball, I told him she called, and I asked if they were still sleeping together, and he said they were and reminded me that what was between us was casual, that he never agreed to an exclusive relationship, that I was moving to Los Angeles, and that he was staying in Houston. But I heard, *I'm madly in love with you, and if we were both moving to Los Angeles, we'd be together forever,* so I had sex with him again and felt a sudden sympathy for Wayne's ex-girlfriend Stacy in the movie *Wayne's World* when she refuses to understand that she and Wayne have broken up. "Happy anniversary, Wayne," she says.

"Stacy, we broke up two months ago," Wayne says.

"That doesn't mean we can't still go out, does it?"

"Well, it does actually," Wayne says. "That's what breaking up is."

. . .

I drove from Dallas to Los Angeles and wasn't quite sure when I arrived because I couldn't find the center of the city. I rented a two-bedroom apartment in Hollywood with a friend from TFA. We lived upstairs from the lead singer of a Journey cover band who had long blond hair and wore white blazers and jeans even when he was not performing. Our address was 508½, and the ½ made me laugh every time I thought about it. I walked around my new neighborhood trying to understand it. There was a garage sale on almost every block, but no one actually had a garage, so the sales happened on people's front lawns, socks and shirts and pants laid carefully over bushes or on blankets spread on the grass, as if people would rather sell their dirty clothes than do laundry.

People in the administrative offices of the Compton Unified School District explained I would have to be drug-tested to teach elementary school with an emergency credential. I was excited. I missed taking tests. "Make sure you drink enough liquid. If you don't pass, you can't teach," they said.

I woke up early the day of the test. I drank two cups of coffee and several cans of Dr Pepper. I brought another can with me to the waiting room. I sipped the brown liquid through a straw and watched people go in and out of the bathroom. Sometimes they came back to the waiting room to drink more water.

The receptionist called my name, and I walked into the bathroom. "Here you go," the woman in the bathroom said and handed me a clear plastic cup with raised lines for measuring. She moved to the corner of the small tiled room and turned her head away from me, which I took as my signal to begin, so I unbuttoned my pants, pushed them to my knees, pulled down my underwear, and sat on the toilet. I knew I was prepared, but I was nervous. I went to Jamaica for spring break during my senior year. I smoked pot and ate Quaker Oats Squares and Starbursts and peanut butter in a bungalow. The people who owned the bungalows wrote messages on our beds every day in fuzzy purple flower petals. *We love you*, they wrote. *Hello pretty American ladies.*

I held the cup under me in the wrong place and peed on my hand. I tightened my muscles, made the necessary adjustments, and filled the cup. But I wasn't finished. I didn't know if I should continue to pee into the cup or move it aside and finish directly in the bowl. They didn't tell me the rules, but I was sure there were rules, so I chose the cup. When my bladder was finally empty, I lifted the cup out from between my legs, held it in my left hand, carefully pulled up my underwear and my pants, and buttoned them, one-handed. Thinking it was the polite thing to do, I wiped off the outside of the cup with a paper towel. Triumphant, I offered the full warm cup to the woman still in the bathroom with me. I extended it toward her, slowly. I didn't want to lose a drop.

She crossed her arms and shook her head. "We don't need that much," she said.

That hadn't occurred to me.

She pointed at the toilet. I turned and dumped some of my urine into the water. I held the cup up for her to examine. She shook her head. "Still too much." I tilted the cup again and then showed it to her. She nodded and took the cup from me and labeled it efficiently.

"You can go," she said.

"That's it?" I asked.

"That's it," she said.

"When will I get the results?" I asked.

She shrugged, and I wanted to ask again, but I held my tongue.

. . .

The school secretary handed me the key to my classroom, and I was a teacher—the bilingual teacher, it turned out, though I could barely speak twenty words in Spanish. My thirty-six first-grade students showed up every morning, smiling, laughing, ready to learn at a school with boarded-up windows, maggots crawling through the classroom floor, dead mice in glue traps behind the empty bookshelves, a playground that was just dirt and sun, falling ceiling tiles and asbestos.

A stray bullet near our school made its way into a third-grade classroom and hit the teacher in the head. He died instantly. One of his students was interviewed on the news. Right before the bullet killed her teacher, he told her she might like to read a book about rocks. "I just want my teacher to come back," she said.

One of my friend's seventh-grade students was sent to a group home for boys because he didn't have a foster home. Another boy there beat him to death with a brick.

My student's uncle was shot while he was washing his car.

Another student's mother hung herself in the bathroom.

In the middle of the day, a student knocked on my classroom door. When I opened it, she said, "Code Yellow," and then ran to the classroom next to mine and knocked on its door, too. Code Yellow meant there was someone near the campus with a gun. It meant I kept my students away from the windows. It meant we kept our heads down. It meant I didn't answer the door, no matter how many times the person knocked or how hard they knocked or how much the person shouted, which posed a problem because the school had no PA system, so the only way to know when *Code Yellow* was over was when someone knocked on the door to tell you.

James Cone's God

What part of humanity is made in the image of God? The part that makes all slaves rebel against their masters. God encounters us as the liberator of the poor, empowering us to fight for freedom because we were made for it.

Love yourself precisely because you are black—and be ready to die if anyone tries to make you believe or behave otherwise. In a racist society, God is never color-blind.

Christianity is a religion of liberation. Any message not related to the liberation of the poor is not Christ's message; any theology indifferent to the theme of liberation is not Christian theology.

Face it: Christ is black. Theology is black. God is black. And this blackness is both a matter of skin color and a matter of ontology—that is to say, blackness is literal blackness, but it is also about the struggle for liberation. Blackness stands for all victims of oppression who realize that the survival of their humanity is bound up with their freedom. To receive God's revelation is to become black with God by joining in the work of liberation.

If God is not for us, if God is not against racists, then God is a murderer, and we had better kill God. This is not a time to be polite. This is a time to speak the truth.

I liked to spend time with the other TFA corps members who were as anxious as I was. I chose my friends by the dark circles under their eyes, by the fact that they too could talk only about how fucked up this whole thing was, about how the world didn't work the way they thought it worked, about how our students were being screwed and how we were part of that screwing, about the myth of meritocracy. "There are no books!" we shouted. "No fucking books in a fucking school!" Most of them were smokers before they arrived in L.A., and the rest of us were now. We looked disoriented, lost, our eyes vacant, unfocused. Some of my friends were so out of it that it was hardly a surprise when one of them killed her cat by accidentally drying him in the dryer.

But my traumatized friends were not the only kind of TFA corps members in Los Angeles. There were those who were not deterred by the lack of desks or books or by their encounters with institutional racism or the violence that is poverty. All impediments made them stronger, more determined—as if injustice could be overcome with just a little extra effort on their parts. They wrote grants and started sports teams and put on dance performances and directed plays after school and then hosted parties on Saturday nights so they could tell the rest of us about the amazing things they were doing. I listened politely and nodded, but all I wanted to do was punch them in the face.

I stopped going to their parties and stayed home alone on Saturday nights instead, staring at the walls. I imagined my apartment when I was not in it. Mattress. Box spring. Folding chairs. Television. I called Austin a few times, and he never called me back. I ate cold soup right out of the can and then felt fat and disgusting because I ate the whole thing and then felt ashamed that I felt fat because I knew some of my students never had enough to eat. They appeared to be starving, their stomachs concave or inflated, their teeth rotting in their mouths.

"Aren't you afraid?" people asked when they found out I taught in Compton. "No," I said. "I'm not afraid," which was a lie because I was afraid, just not of the people the questioners assumed I should be.

In *On Beauty and Being Just*, Elaine Scarry uses a poem by Emily Dickinson to describe what it feels like to make a perceptual error about the world around you—to believe something is beautiful and then discover it is not beautiful at all, to believe something is right and just and then discover it is not right or just at all:

It dropped so low—in my Regard—
I heard it hit the Ground—
And go to pieces on the Stones
at the bottom of my mind.

Change makes a loud sound, like a plate dropped on a hard floor.

I signed up for Teach for America because I wanted to help people, because I wanted to save people. But if there was any saving going on in my classroom, it was of me. It was *from* me.

I went to a fast-food restaurant after school to get something to eat. The bulletproof glass was thick between me and the person taking my order. I had to speak loudly to make myself heard. "A small order of fries and a Dr Pepper please," I said, sliding my money through the narrow slot at the bottom of the window. She entered my order into her register and slid my change back to me.

"What are you doing here?" she asked.

. . .

When word travels that Jesus is home, so many people come to his house that there's no room for them—not even in the doorway—but people keep coming. One group brings a friend who is paralyzed. They can't carry him into the house because of the crowds, so they remove the roof.

I was looking for a roof to dig my way through, and I was looking for someone who might be willing to lower me down. I lay still on my mat in the middle of the floor and looked up at the stars. I waited for the moon, for something to rise.

My bedroom was filled with candles—votives and pillars stuck in glass bowls and ceramic candleholders and perforated tin boxes. I couldn't stop buying them.

The light shines in the darkness, and the darkness did not overcome it, I thought as I struck each match trying to light up what was growing inside me.

I introduced myself to men at bars or on the beach or in my neighborhood. We exchanged phone numbers. They promised to call. I imagined our future, how we'd tell our children it was love at first sight, how we knew the minute we saw each other that we were meant to be together. I sat by the phone. I picked it up occasionally to make sure there was a dial tone. I decided to call them because *I'm a modern woman who doesn't need to wait for men to call me.* On the phone—once I reminded them who I was—we arranged to have lunch or get a cup of coffee or a beer. I hung up and scheduled a haircut. Bought a new shirt or skirt or dress. Sometimes, we actually went on a date and the silence between us filled up with the realization that we had nothing in common. Other times they called an hour or so before we were scheduled to meet, and I answered the phone, sitting on the edge of my bed in my new shirt or skirt or dress, loving my new haircut. "Something came up at the last minute," they said.

I turned my attention away from strangers and toward the men I saw in my daily life. I had a crush on the man behind the counter at the bagel shop I went to every morning on my way to school. He handed me my coffee. Our fingers touched. I could tell he liked me.

We spent several weeks staring at each other over the counter, and then I said, "We should do something sometime." He wrote his beeper number on a napkin and handed it to me.

I beeped him, and he called me back, and I found myself in the front seat of his pickup truck barreling down the highway to a dance club somewhere outside of Los Angeles. I had no idea where we were, and if I focused on that I felt panicky. So I didn't think about it or about the fact that I was wearing a really short skirt in the front seat of a pickup truck with a man whose last name I didn't know, and who would only give me his beeper number, and who was wearing a gold band on his left ring finger that he insisted was a gift from his father, and not a wedding ring. We arrived at the club, and we danced to loud music, and in the pulsing light he pushed me up against one of the poles in the middle of the dance floor and rubbed my ass. Later he drove me home. We kissed. He sucked on my toes.

Next, Kinko's. I stopped at the copy shop every day because my school in Compton only had one copy machine and the women in the front office discouraged teachers from using it. "Thirty copies?" the man behind the counter asked when I handed him a stack of worksheets, and I thought, *he knows me, he really, really knows me.*

"Thirty-six," I said and smiled.

"You can wait or you can pick them up tomorrow," he said, and I knew he wanted me to wait.

"I'll wait," I said, and he turned and walked away, and I wandered around the store pretending to be interested in the displays of plastic binders and report covers and file folders. I knew the fluorescent lighting wasn't good for my complexion, but I tried to stay in his line of sight even though his back was to me.

My mother visited my classroom and brought every one of my thirty-six students a book, wrapped in tissue paper, tied with ribbon. Some of my students were so excited to have a new book that belonged to them that they started to cry.

I took my mother to a play in downtown Los Angeles that night, and on the ride home, we saw a dead body covered with a sheet in the middle of the highway. "What kind of place is this?" she asked.

. . .

Sunday morning she took me to All Saints, an Episcopal church in Pasadena. It was a rock service, and there was a band at the front of the sanctuary. Drums. Electric guitars. Microphones. Amplifiers. The rector, Ed Bacon, stood at the top of the steps that led to the altar and invited everyone to Communion, saying, "This table is the center of our lives. Whoever you are and wherever you find yourself on your journey of faith, you are welcome here."

God didn't become human to prove how wretched we are, one of the priests said, but to help us remember how hallowed and blessed human life and experiences are. He said: Think of the Bible as a whole. It tells us that God and human beings are connected to one another. It tells us about God's concrete involvement in daily life. It tells us that God takes human life seriously, and if God takes human life seriously, then God takes your life seriously. If God is present in Jesus, then God can be present in you.

The power of the resurrection, he said, is that God stays with us after all the pain, after the betrayal, the suffering, the violence, the denial. Not even that can stop God from wanting to connect with us. God will not let us go.

A few Sundays later, at the newcomers' meeting after church, I sat in a small room with other people new to All Saints and couldn't stop crying long enough to introduce myself. "Don't worry," the woman leading the meeting said. "This happens all the time."

Desmond Tutu's God

God holds the victim of violence in God's hands and weeps, saying, "You, you, you. I made you."

And then God holds the perpetrator of violence and, again, God weeps. "You, you, you. I made you."

I fell in love with God at All Saints. I'd never fallen in love with someone who was also in love with me. I always fell in love with men I didn't know or who told me again and again they were unavailable or who were dating other women or who couldn't remember my name or who didn't really know anything about me because I turned myself into the person I imagined they wanted me to be. I *loved* loving people who didn't love me. I loved trying to make them fall in love with me. I loved that they never did.

This time was different. I was Molly Ringwald in *Sixteen Candles* with Jake Ryan sitting cross-legged on my dining room table and leaning over the candles glowing on my birthday cake to kiss me. If God wore jeans, we would've had our hands in each other's back pockets. He would've waited for me by my locker.

I also fell in love with All Saints. With all of it. Music. Liturgy. People spilling into the aisles and crawling over pews to share peace with one another. Female priests celebrating Communion. Sermons. The lawn covered with rainbow flags and red ribbons and fliers about protests and marches on city hall. My friends saved me a seat on Sunday mornings, right up front, on the left side of the church, near the altar. People knew what was going on in my life. They prayed for me, prayed for my students, let me cry, brought me soup when I had the flu, sent me home with hot toddies after night meetings when I had a sore throat—individual mason jars filled with lemon, honey, hot tea, and bourbon wrapped in dish towels in a grocery bag in the back seat of my car. I belonged. I knew all the words to the prayers. I knew all the songs. I sang along with the choir. When the priest dismissed the congregation at the end of a church service one Sunday she said, "We are home," and I knew it was true.

I had moved to Venice to live near the beach with a friend from college named Yuki, but I drove almost an hour to Pasadena to go to All Saints three times a week—to church services and evening classes and leaders' workshops and guest speaker series. If you'd mapped my life during this time, you would've seen me repeatedly drive legs of the same triangular pilgrimage: Venice to Compton, Compton to Pasadena, Pasadena to Venice, Venice to Pasadena, Pasadena to Compton. The 105, the 110, the 10. Home to school, school to church, church to home.

I was waking up, becoming aware of my complicity in oppression, realizing I had benefited from the very system that was harming my students in Compton. "We did this!" I kept shouting to anyone who would listen. "This is not an accident!" I felt like one of the houses cut in half by the artist Gordon Matta-Clark, split open, exposed, and that feeling brought me to All Saints week after week, to the promise of a God whose love could save, a God I gave myself to completely, the surrender a relief. I was not in charge, God was in charge, and God was love and wanted the best for everyone, but our greed and insecurity and grabbing fear and small-mindedness and short-sightedness created injustice. My new faith was part belief in human agency—*God has no other hands on earth than ours*—and part withdrawal, submission—*into God's hands I commend my spirit.*

I was given multiple copies of the *Book of Common Prayer*, big leather volumes I stacked by my bed with lots of ribbons to mark my place. "God really loves you, Sarah," my friends said.

"I know," I said, smiling.

I talked to God all the time. I prayed during the day in my classroom, at night while I drove on highways, on weekend mornings while I Rollerbladed on the beach. I recited "Night Prayer" from the *New Zealand Prayer Book* every night. *For those beloved of God are given gifts even while they sleep,* I said and felt blessed to have found a God who loved me all the time, even when I was asleep. I couldn't get enough of God. *God be with me. God within me. God beside me. God before me. God to comfort and restore me. God beneath me. God above me. God in hearts of all that love me,* I sang again and again, and I could feel him everywhere.

A Romantic's God

You who reject religion, Friedrich Schleiermacher writes, you who despise it, you do not see the true essence of religion. What you hate is merely the husk. Let me peel it back. Let me show you what's inside.

The primary human experience is the feeling of utter dependence—that is what it means to be human. We are not fully autonomous, we are not absolutely free, and we know it, every day, every minute, every second of our lives. Listen: That feeling is the same as being in relation with God. We can never really forget God because the feeling of God is always inside us, waiting to be remembered.

Yuki and I lived less than a mile from Maylen, one of my roommates from college. Maylen was reading *The*

Artist's Way by Julia Cameron. "I think you'd love this book," she said. "I think it would change your life."

"But I'm not an artist," I said. "I'm not even creative."

"Everyone's creative," Maylen said. "Julia Cameron says people who surround themselves with artists want to be artists themselves. Think about it. Then call me back."

I couldn't draw. I didn't paint. I took piano lessons for twelve years, but I could barely play. I believed creativity was innate, people either had it or they didn't, and I didn't—but I wanted to. I drove to the bookstore and bought the book.

Cameron believes we are victims of our own internalized perfectionist, a critic she calls the Censor. The Censor talks constantly, an expert at convincing you she has your best interest at heart. She's keeping you safe. Knows what's good for you. Cameron asks that you write "morning pages," three pages, by hand, every single day. There's no wrong way to write these pages. Nothing's too petty or silly or stupid or weird. Just get the Censor out of your head and onto the page.

I started writing morning pages, and my Censor wasted no time showing up: *The Artist's Way? You think you're an artist? You want to paint? Just like you wanted to take jazz when you were in second grade? Why don't you just put on a tutu and dance around on the Venice boardwalk? Silly girl. Who do you think you are? You can't write and you definitely can't paint. You don't even know how to draw. You suck at the piano and you took lessons for twelve years! And do I need to mention how ungrateful you are? How ugly? And fat? And lazy? You can't even get out of bed in the morning the first time your alarm goes off, and you think you're going to make something beautiful? Please. Don't make me laugh. Please.*

I once heard that to try to understand what their patients with schizophrenia experience, some psychiatrists wear headphones. At coffee shops, in meetings with colleagues, in playrooms with children, on subway cars, voices shout through the headphones, saying how stupid the psychiatrists are or that they're being followed or that the world will be better without them in it or that other people aren't even real.

I didn't need headphones.

"Most people can't see who Jesus really is," Tim Safford, a priest at All Saints, said in a sermon before Christmas. "Not the disciples, not people from his hometown, not the leaders of his synagogue." Jesus goes to Galilee. A man possessed by a demon sees him. *Let us alone!* the demon shouts. *Have you come to destroy us? I know who you are, the Holy One of God.*

"Our demons recognize Jesus," Tim said. Not our angels. Not what's good and kind and generous in us, but what's greedy, needy, stuck, petty, full of judgment. What's most afraid. "Those are the parts of us that know who Jesus is. And they know following Jesus means the end of them. So they shout at him. Try to make him go away. But what they really want is to be healed."

My Censor tried to protect me. She showed me how to play it safe, how to hide the parts of me other people wouldn't like, how to be good. She was preemptive: she shamed me to keep me from being shamed by others.

I went to a workshop on prayer at All Saints, and the leader of the workshop, Anne Peterson, said, "God loves us as we are, not as we wish we were." Prayer isn't about being perfect, she told us. It's not about letting God see only the parts of us that are good. It's about believing God wants to see all of us—about believing God loves all of us—especially the parts we're not proud of. "We don't pray to make God love us," Anne said. "We pray to respond to the love of God that is already being offered to us. Prayer is about falling in love with the God who is already in love with us."

I thought of Dupré's class and how he said that true love is loving *what remains when all that beauty is gone, when all that is left is bareness.* I had made my life a spectacle, something for people to marvel at. *Let what I do be pleasing in Thy sight.* I had been waiting for applause. But now I heard something different. *Lay your burden down.*

Pretending to be the person I thought other people needed me to be—the person I thought God needed me to be—was a kind of lie. It was deceitful and manipulative. Dishonest. The good things I did in the world had an ugly underside: I didn't do them for others. I did them for myself. I did them to make people love me.

"We don't have to have everything just right to pray," Anne said. "We just have to tell the truth. If we can't be honest with God, we can't be honest with anyone."

What do honest prayers sound like? I asked myself.

I answered my own question: *They sound like morning pages.*

I started writing back to the Censor. When I read my morning pages from that time now, a new kind of God seems to be waging war with my Censor on the page: *You are ugly. You are lazy.* You are my beloved. *You're wasting your life. You should be ashamed.* With you I am well pleased.

Shut up, I wrote. SHUT THE FUCK UP.

Be silent, Jesus says to the demons. *Come out.*

. . .

My group of friends at All Saints consisted of the people who led the small group programs, and it felt to me like an inner circle, but there was also an inner-inner circle—the people called to be priests. Being called granted them special status—private meetings with the priests on staff, extra responsibilities, exclusive committees, an aura of holiness as if God had reached down from heaven and tapped them on the shoulder. *You*, I imagined he said. *I want you*.

People told me I had spiritual gifts, that I was called to the priesthood, and I wanted it to be true. I craved the outward sign, the blessing of the community, the special mark. Better to choose the prepackaged, the ready-made. Better to stick with the script.

It was the middle of my second year of teaching in Compton, the end of my commitment with Teach for America, and I didn't yet have another job or any idea what to do next. I had never intended to be a teacher. My plan had been to teach for two years and then go to graduate school in comparative literature, but I didn't want to do that anymore. It felt irrelevant. It felt like running away.

Offer your life as a living sacrifice to God, the priests said every Sunday before Communion. I wanted to know how to do that.

When I was alone, and when I could shut my Censor up for half a second, I could hear a quiet voice whisper to me, *Write,* but almost as soon as I heard that voice, my Censor drowned it out: *And how will you make money? And what do you think you have to say? And what good would that do your students in Compton?*

One Sunday, Ed Bacon gave a sermon on vocation. "There is the moment when you are born, and there is another moment when you figure out why," he said.

"Your vocational identity is etched deep inside you." Then he told a story: He was studying to be a lawyer, and in the middle of an exam, he realized he was called to be a minister. He put down his pen, stood up, and walked out of the room.

I wanted to stand up in the middle of an exam. I wanted to walk out of a room. I wanted God to tell me what to do.

By the time I arrived at All Saints, I had lived most of my life trying to be the person I thought other people wanted me to be because I believed that was the only way I would ever be loved. People wouldn't love the real me. They'd only love the me I created for them. Loneliness. Isolation.

All Saints offered me a way out of this. *God loves you God loves you God loves you*, I heard every single Sunday. The priests promised God loved me exactly as I was, with all my flaws and failings and shortcomings. God loved the secret me I hadn't shared with anyone—the me who lived somewhere hidden, buried under all those other selves.

I had been a costumed marionette with strings I handed over to other people, and I think people at All Saints were trying to tell me I could take the strings back. But I didn't. I handed them over to God.

Your will, your will, your will, I wrote again and again in my journal.

. . .

I applied for two jobs, one in Dallas teaching at a private middle school, and another in Los Angeles working with a nun directing a welfare-to-work program at a hospital.

The principal in Dallas took me on a tour of the new middle school building and showed me unlocked cabinets full of paper and loose-leaf binders and pens and Magic Markers, which made me cry—especially the dozen rolls of butcher paper lined up against the wall. I had to buy most things for my classroom in Compton—books, watercolors, crayons, paper, pencils, folders—and barter with the man guarding the supply closet, trading Skittles or M&M's or Tootsie Pops for what little else the school had. I cried so hard that the principal opened her purse and handed me a tissue. Then she wrote me a check. "For your students," she said.

During my interview at the hospital, I followed the nun through hallways that smelled like Band-Aids and gauze. Her shoes made no sound on the slick shiny floors. The job paid well—much better than teaching—and before the end of the interview, I'd already decided how to spend my first paycheck.

I was offered both jobs, but I didn't want either one. I asked Tim Safford what I should do. "To make a decision, you have to know what you want," he said. "And you have to believe that what you want is important.

That's the task of discernment: to believe you are important enough to listen to, to believe you are important enough—just as you are—that God will speak to you."

I remembered a college counselor at my high school telling my brother to be like an onion—to let his insides determine what the outside looks like. *But what if there's nothing on the inside?* I thought.

I'd been writing the same words in my morning pages every day for months: *I don't want to take the job in Dallas, and I don't want to take the job with the nun. I want to write about my students. I want to paint. I will ask Maylen to take me to the art supply store.* And the next morning: *I don't want to take the job in Dallas, and I don't want to take the job with the nun. I want to write about my students. I want to paint. I will ask Maylen to take me to the art supply store.* Amnesia. I forgot what I wrote as soon as I closed my journal.

I learned at church that there are two words for life in Greek: *bios*, the word for ordinary, day-to-day life, and *zoe*, the word for life itself, God's life, abundant life, eternal life. Communion is the daily, weekly movement from *bios* to *zoe*, and it is a sacrament in the Episcopal Church, a bridge that anchors the invisible, transcendent, intangible God in the visible, tangible world. Communion is anti-amnesia, an *anamnesis* according to Kenneth Leech—literally a loss of forgetfulness. It is supposed to help us remember that we are

Jesus's resurrected body. When we eat the bread and drink the wine, Jesus is *re-membered*, his body put back together.

Every Sunday at All Saints we recited the same prayers, read the same book, sang the same songs, ate the same bread, drank the same wine. Jesus is born. Jesus dies. Jesus rises from the dead. Jesus is born. Jesus dies. Jesus rises from the dead. *Crucify him! Crucify him!* we shouted every year during the Passion play, as if we'd forgotten he's the son of God, as if we'd forgotten we were killing the very thing that might save us.

I called the middle school and said no.

I called the nun. "I'd like to accept your offer," I said.

"You're too late," she said. "I gave the job to someone else."

Thank you thank you thank you.

I called Maylen and asked her to take me to the art supply store. We walked through the aisles, and she explained which canvases and brushes and acrylic paint to buy. She drove me home, helped me carry my new tools into my apartment, gave me a hug, and left.

Alone in the middle of my living room I looked around. I chose a canvas. I dipped a paintbrush in a pot of orange and painted a horizontal stripe across the top of the canvas. I dipped another brush in red and painted a stripe of red underneath the orange. Then green, yellow, black, blue, purple, white. I filled the canvas with lines of color, and when I reached the bottom, I started at the top again, my canvas thick with paint.

I'd been reading a book of poems by Lucille Clifton. I'd memorized "i am not done yet" and wanted to eat the words. *Open your mouth and eat what I give you*, God says, and Ezekiel eats the scroll.

I found a knife in the kitchen and used it to carve Clifton's words into the paint. When I finished, I painted over the words with more stripes of color and wrote the same words again. I painted like the monks who wrote new holy words on top of older ones they partially erased. Their parchments contain layers and layers of text. Some words are legible and some are not, but reading the words is not the point. Writing is all that matters. You write the words to become the words, as if you'd swallowed them, sweet as honey.

. . .

I went to church on the Thursday before Easter, Maundy Thursday, the last supper, the night Jesus washed his disciples' feet, the night we would wash one another's feet. In an alcove of the sanctuary was a chair, a basin of water, a stack of towels. When I reached the front of the line, the woman in front of me sat in the chair. I was on my knees. Her bare feet in warm water. My hands holding the soles of her feet, my hands pouring warm water over her feet, my hands drying her feet with a towel, until it was my turn to sit in the chair, to let the person behind me hold, wash, dry.

At the end of the service on Good Friday, the sanctuary was stripped—flowers, candles, tablecloths, everything removed until there was only a cross, draped in purple cloth, and a single candle. People took shifts watching over that one light, guarding it so it wouldn't go out. My watch was in the middle of the night on Holy Saturday, four of the hours between Jesus's death and resurrection, hours I imagined even Jesus didn't know whether he would rise.

What if the gospels ended differently? What if there were no gardener, no man in a white robe shining, no road to Emmaus, no angels, no upper room? What if we weren't waiting for him to come back?

Offer your life as a living sacrifice.

I would write a book about my students. I would be a priest.

. . .

To make money while I wrote about my students and applied for divinity school, I worked at the coffee shop down the street from my apartment. My boss, Sonny, loved to tell customers I was going to be a priest, and when I was running the blender to make a smoothie and couldn't hear them, they'd ask her all sorts of questions about my life. "Don't worry," Sonny said when they left. "I tell all the men who ask about you that you don't have sex or drink alcohol or date."

I wore my self on the outside, dressing it up for people to see and admire. Saying *I'm going to be a priest* was part of this costume, a badge, a mask. Just being me wasn't enough. I needed props.

Other twenty-three-year-olds I knew didn't want to be priests, and that was, at least in part, why I chose the vocation. Wanting to be a priest marked me as different, and being different felt like being chosen. "You're going to be a priest?" people asked, and like all good prophets at the moment of their calling, I feigned humility, looked down at the ground, shuffled my feet, acted embarrassed by all the attention. I imagined myself like Jonah in the belly of a whale. *Here I am. Send me.*

4

MOVING IN TOGETHER

THAT FIRST SEPTEMBER at Harvard Divinity School, I found myself surrounded by other people—many of them also in their twenties—who wanted to be ministers, but my newfound community didn't take away from my feeling of being chosen. It heightened it. We were a tribe.

The divinity school occupies two buildings at the far end of Harvard's campus. Before its most recent renovation, Andover Hall seemed to face away from the rest of the campus as if it had turned its back on the school's secular ways in frustration, its front door opening to a leafy residential street instead. Plaques in

Divinity Hall marked places where famous people slept or ate or preached, and some of the toilets were made by a company called Church, which made going to the bathroom feel alternately holy and sacrilegious.

My new apartment was on a tree-lined boulevard with Fresh Pond on one end and Mount Auburn Cemetery on the other. I imagined God and I were moving in together: We unpacked our boxes, deciding whose rice cooker or toaster or blender to keep and whose to give away. We hung my paintings around the house and put photographs in frames, and on one wall of my study we arranged a display of crosses people gave me when they learned I was headed to divinity school to become a priest—ceramic crosses hand-painted with miniature houses and trees and people, crosses carved out of stone, crosses made out of wood and hammered tin. We ate every meal together. We talked deep into the night.

The master of divinity program is the three-year degree for people who want to become leaders in their faith traditions—ministers, priests, monks, rabbis, imams. There were students from all different faith traditions—Christians and Jews and Muslims and Buddhists and Sikhs and Hindus—and there were also agnostics and students with no religious faith—atheists, humanists. We had all come to school to talk about religion—what it is, why it matters, how it works—and to think critically about how it functions in the world. And we did, in the hallways after class, in the communal kitchen in the basement of the dorms, in the refectory during lunch, over beers at bars in Harvard Square.

I was in Cambridge to go to Harvard Divinity School, to become a priest, but when I moved there, I stopped going to church. Now this fact jumps off the page like a warning signal, all bright lights and flashing, but at the time I didn't think much of it. I felt like I was living, breathing, and eating God. I didn't need to go somewhere special on Sunday mornings to be with him.

I did attend the weekly chapel service at the divinity school on Wednesdays, and I also made a few haphazard attempts to find a faith community in Cambridge, but I was longing for All Saints, and my yearning for that place blinded me to what the churches I visited had to offer. It was as if I couldn't see the nice people who approached me at coffee hour or delivered homemade bread to my door or invited me to join book groups. Their churches didn't look like All Saints or smell like All Saints or sound like All Saints. They weren't using inclusive language or blessing same-sex unions. I gave each congregation one chance to impress me and then wrote the place off.

I was a future priest who didn't go to church—a detail that should have made me nervous—but many of the friends I made at divinity school didn't go to church either, so my free time on Sunday mornings wasn't remarkable. Some of my friends worked at churches, although working at a church and attending church aren't the same. Getting paid to be there changes everything.

I didn't want to be a parishioner. I wanted to be a priest. I was caught in a liminal space between being someone who attends church and someone who runs one, and if I couldn't be in charge of what was happening on Sunday morning, I didn't want any part of it. What led me to the priesthood in the first place was the clear role that comes with wearing a clerical collar. I wanted to be the shepherd, not the flock.

As a teenager, I sometimes fantasized about shaving off my blond hot-rolled hair, piercing my ears and nose and lip, tattooing all visible skin. I imagined the relief that would come with that outward display, the clarity of it. *This is who I am. This is where I belong. These are my people.* Being a priest offered something similar, a way to be done with the messy work of crafting an identity, a way out of gray and into black and white. I would be chosen, worthy, loved. I would be the bride of God.

. . .

I was familiar with many biblical stories, but I had almost no experience with the book as a whole, and until I had to buy one for class, I didn't own a Bible. I don't remember there being Bibles in the pews at All

Saints, which doesn't mean they weren't there, just that I never actually opened one in church. All the passages I needed were printed in the weekly program.

In Introduction to Hebrew Scriptures, the professor called out passages for us to analyze during class. "Please turn to First Samuel 16:4," he said, and I thought, *Shit! There's more than one Samuel?* I watched the students next to me and used the thickness of the pages on either side of the opening in their Bibles to determine where I ought to begin my search. Luckily I wasn't the only one in the room rifling anxiously through the loud thin pages. "I can see you Episcopalians from here," the professor said and shook his head.

Someone during orientation told me David Lamberth was a great professor, so I enrolled in Introduction to Theological Thinking, a class held in a room with bad acoustics, uncomfortable desks, and wildly fluctuating temperatures. None of that mattered. I loved his class. Lamberth threw around the names of theologians and philosophers I'd never heard of, but I was too embarrassed to raise my hand and ask who they were because everyone else in the room seemed to be nodding in recognition, so I wrote their names phonetically in my notes and then rushed to the library to look them up, a hard thing to do when you've misspelled what you're trying to find. He used words like *hermeneutics* and *ontology* and *deontological* and *epistemological* and *kerygmatic* as if he were saying *chair* and *desk* and *window* and *tree* and *book*. I spent a lot of time searching through the thick dictionaries stacked on top of the bookcases in the library, and it was often the shortest words that proved most difficult—words like *qua*, a Latin word that means "as" that Lamberth used at least once each class. "He's making an argument about being *qua* being," Lamberth would say about a particular theologian, and I'm still not sure exactly what he meant.

In his class, I studied Freidrich Schleiermacher's feeling of "utter dependence," Martin Luther's belief that to fulfill the law you had to love the law, Gotthold Ephraim Lessing's "ditch," Martin Buber's *I and Thou*, Paul Tillich's "ultimate concern," and Gordon Kaufman's "serendipitous creativity." I was dizzied by deconstructionists' meditations on presence and absence, appearance and disappearance. I learned about feminist and womanist and black and liberation theologians—Elisabeth Schüssler Fiorenza writing women back into the biblical text and Kelly Brown Douglas revealing the blackness of Christ and Gustavo Gutiérrez asserting that to be Christian means to live in solidarity with the oppressed and Cornel West insisting it was time to stop thinking about whether or not something is theological enough and start worrying about whether or not it makes a difference in the world.

Some theologians we studied believed the words they wrote about God were dictated to them by God, revealed. Others believed the words they wrote about God were human words, products of their imaginations, constructions. But almost all of the theologians we read agreed that the language people use to talk about God is special, powerful language that shapes how people move through the world. An essential element of the theological task was ethical—to determine what was required of human beings, to figure out how people ought to live. At the end of every class, Lamberth asked, "So, what's the cash value?" He was asking us to think about what difference ideas about God make, and more than anything else it was this idea—that our thinking about God has real effects on the world—that made me want to study theology.

Although I had known, of course, that there were different religions and that each claimed different deities or different ways of understanding the divine, I hadn't known there was such a variety of thinking about God in Christianity itself. The previous extent of my theological knowledge came from what I'd managed to piece together in Sunday school, classrooms at Yale, and in pews at All Saints, and it all revolved around a God we called Father who had a son we called Jesus Christ who died and rose to save all believers. I knew there were gospel writers and saints and priests and mystics, but I didn't know there were people in the world called theologians, and I definitely didn't know that most of the philosophers I'd studied in college—Kant, Hegel, Kierkegaard, Nietzsche—wrote so much about God.

Theology—*theos* (God) and *logos* (word)—means words about God. The ancient Greeks called the theologian a "poet who speaks of God." For me, studying theology felt like reading love poems, lyrical descriptions of what it feels like to look out at the universe and feel loved and saved and held. I read the assigned texts with the same devotion I'd had when listening to love songs in middle school. Play. Rewind. Play again. God was singing to me through those texts, and their writers understood me, knew how it felt to promise your life to someone, to be known.

But it was in Lamberth's class that a canyon began to open between the God I was in love with and the God I was studying. The God I was in love with—the God who stayed with me through the night, who knit me in my mother's womb, who chose me, saw me, made me, knew me, called me beloved—was different from the God I read about in theologians' texts. I didn't, at first, see the chasm open, the fracture form and spread, and even if I had, I don't think I would have considered it a problem. It was good for our relationship, invigorating. I was getting to know God by spending time with his closest friends, and even though the stories they told about him made me wonder who this God really was, I told myself that what I was learning about God only made our love stronger, more real. I had long suspected that there was more to God than I had been told in church, and the theologians' texts confirmed my suspicion. God was greater than I had ever imagined. Loving God could change the world.

When I was in second grade, my homeroom teacher, Mr. Hornbach, asked us how long we thought the dashed lines that separated lanes of traffic were. "One foot?" we guessed. "Two feet?" He recorded our estimates, lined us up, and walked us across the campus to look at the road that ran in front of our school. We stood on the sidewalk while Mr. Hornbach lay down in the middle of the street next to the painted white line. The line was longer than his body. Much longer. We gasped. He stood and took a tape measure from his pocket. We counted with him as he laid the tape down. *One two three four five six seven eight nine ten.* Ten feet! *What we think we see is not what we see. What we think we know is not all there is to know.* Everything was possible. Everything was up for grabs.

In Lamberth's class I watched theologians lay their bodies down. *See?* they said.

. . .

The seminar I took with Gordon Kaufman met on the first floor of Divinity Hall around a table as long and narrow as a canoe. Kaufman sat at the helm, his knit wool bag—a gift from one of his daughters—laid across the table or hung over the back of his chair.

During the first class, Kaufman asked students to describe a religious experience they have had. "I experience God when I'm in nature," one student said.

"Say more," Kaufman said. "What do you mean when you say that?"

"When I'm walking in the woods, and I hear the leaves crunching under my feet, and I smell the trees, and I look at the blue sky, that's a religious experience."

"Why do you call it a religious experience?" Kaufman asked.

"I feel at peace."

"What makes that feeling *religious*?" Kaufman asked.

"I feel a sense of oneness."

"And what makes that feeling *religious*?" Kaufman asked.

"I feel connected to everything that is."

"What I am trying to ask is this: Why do you call walking in the woods a religious experience? What is it about peace or oneness or feeling connected that is inherently religious?"

No one spoke.

"Don't you call those feelings religious because someone told you that religious experiences include feelings of peace and oneness and connection?" Kaufman asked. There is no such thing as raw, unmediated experience, he explained. Our experiences are shaped by the language we use to name them, dependent on terms and concepts that we've learned, which then give our experiences their particular flavor and shape.

In all of his writings, Kaufman argues that the words we use to talk about God are *human* words, infected with our limitations, interests, and biases. Theologians must write about God knowing what they write might be wrong. They must be relentlessly critical of their faith. Kaufman takes God's mystery seriously, believes God is fundamentally beyond our comprehension. As a result, theology is—and always has been—what he calls "imaginative construction," people putting together a picture of what it means to be human in the world under God. *Stretch a canvas. Paint something new.*

I knew there was a difference between the word and the thing itself, and it made sense to me that this difference would be greatest when it came to God. If God is by definition transcendent—if God is beyond human knowledge, if God is more than anything we can say or think or believe about God—then the study of God must always be incomplete, mysterious. *If you think you know God, it is not God that you know.* But Kaufman turned the theological project upside down for me. He changed its direction: Instead of theology moving from God to humans, theology moves from humans to God. In other words, I heard Kaufman saying, there is no such thing as revelation. There is only what we make. God is not shooting arrows down at us. We are shooting arrows up to God, trying to reach God even as we know our arrows will never hit the mark. Theology is not about getting God right, not about arriving at the Truth, not about receiving information about the real God during a mountaintop experience. It's about looking around at the world and seeing what it needs. About confronting injustice and environmental degradation and poverty and racism and sexism and the possibility of nuclear annihilation and saying, *I can create a version of God that can respond to this.*

When I was with Kaufman, letting go of revelation and claiming theology as a constructive enterprise didn't feel like loss. It felt like liberation, like invitation. I could see that admitting that our words about God are our words about God—that they are made, not found—would make it possible to take responsibility for those words and how they're used. We are carpenters, not marionettes.

Theology wasn't an abstract discipline. It was a pragmatic enterprise that had to do with discovering what's required for living a moral life. What mattered was not the creeds people confess but how they live. "The central question for theology . . . is a *practical* question," Kaufman writes. "How are we to live? To what should we devote ourselves? To what causes give ourselves?" Theology that does not contribute significantly to struggles against inhumanity and injustice, he argues, has lost sight of its point of being.

"Are you saying that God doesn't exist?" one of my classmates asked.

"I'm saying that's not the right question," Kaufman said.

"What do you mean?"

"The question of God's existence will not get you very far. It's a question human beings can't answer. But the word *God* is operating in the world, and when you ask, 'Does God exist?' you have already spoken the word *God*, so God in some sense already exists. The symbol is very much alive."

Kaufman grew up in a Mennonite home and community and is an ordained Mennonite minister. His worldview was shaped by three of Jesus's teachings: love your neighbor as yourself; love your enemies; and live without doing violence, even in the face of death. Kaufman believes human relationships should always be loving—even with your enemies, especially with your enemies. During World War II, he was a conscientious objector.

Kaufman's father was a missionary in China, and part of his father's work there was to officiate at funerals. Kaufman told me that his father always followed the wishes of the people he buried, orienting their bodies east-west, with their heads at the eastern end of the grave, according to their custom. His father's supervisor, however, believed that Christians had to be buried with their heads at the western end of the grave. So after the funerals, against the wishes of the dead person and his or her family, the supervisor would exhume the bodies Kaufman's father had buried, turn them around, and bury them again.

"You're saying God doesn't exist," my classmate said again.

"No, I'm not," Kaufman said. "I'm saying that's not the right question. I'm saying you need to ask yourself what kind of God you want to believe in. I'm saying you need to ask yourself what kind of world you want to live in."

"But you're calling God an imaginative construction," another classmate said. "Doesn't that mean that God is somehow less than real?"

"Everything that matters to us has been imagined," Kaufman said. "There is an imaginative element built into our very selfhood, into our notion of the world and the universe, into every image and idea we use to make our way through life. We create a map with the system of ideas that we come to hold—about the planet, about other people, about what is important, about what is real and what is illusory, about how to comport ourselves, about what is worth doing—and we use that map to find our place in the world, to orient us in the world. Without that map, we couldn't live."

For me, at least intellectually, calling God an imaginative construction didn't make God less than God. It let God be God, beyond human words and comprehension, beyond our finitude and biases and small-mindedness and fear. I understood this way of thinking about God to be a useful way to stop religious violence: if you admit your understanding of God is a construction, then you won't be willing to kill anyone over it. *You could be wrong. You could be wrong. You could be wrong.*

People in the seminar said they were afraid that this kind of thinking led to relativism, that it would be impossible to know right from wrong, good from bad, true from false, but Kaufman thought their fear rested on a misunderstanding of God. Faith in God doesn't make you sure, he said. It doesn't confirm absolutes. It does the opposite: relativizes, raises questions, reminds you that you are human, finite, fallible.

In his book *In Face of Mystery,* Kaufman quotes the Jewish philosopher Martin Buber in a passage that I think reveals why Kaufman is a theologian, why he continues to wrestle with God. "God is the most heavy-laden of all human words," Buber writes. "None has become so soiled, so mutilated. Just for this reason I may not abandon it. Generations . . . have laid the burden of their anxious lives upon this word and weighed it to the ground; it lies in the dust and bears their whole burden. [Humans] with their religious factions have torn the word to pieces; they have killed for it and died for it, and it bears their fingermarks and their blood . . . But we may not give it up . . . We cannot cleanse the word 'God' and we cannot make it whole; but, defiled and mutilated as it is, we can raise it from the ground and set it over an hour of great care."

I can picture Kaufman now: I imagine him standing on a hillside in China where his father once stood. He picks up his shovel. He gently turns the body back around.

I took almost every class Kaufman taught while I was at Harvard, and in that first seminar room, around that table shaped like a boat, I decided I didn't just want to study theology—I wanted to be a theologian. Theology as Kaufman described it was a creative, imaginative, ethical discipline. It was about making words about God matter, about making the world a better place, about turning bodies around. It was about constructing new symbols for God, and I wanted to participate in that work.

But the canyon that had opened in Lamberth's class grew wider. In my consciousness, the idea took root that human beings make gods, and that these gods then make us—shape how we live and who we love, who we'll accept and who we'll cast out. I could see that people have always fashioned gods to serve their needs, to bless what they thought needed blessing, to curse what they thought needed cursing. They have created gods to save them, and they have also created gods to justify destroying others.

And I began to suspect that I was no different. I had forged the ideal God for me—a man in the sky who watched over me, who cherished me and chose me, who judged me and loved me and accepted me, a version of the perfect parent combined with the best boyfriend ever. *You are my beloved, with you I am well pleased.* And I began to wonder if that version of God existed only in my head. It was one thing to see other people's gods as imaginative constructions. It was another to see my God that way. I didn't want Snuffleupagus. I was too old for imaginary friends.

Loving another person is always an exercise in fiction. You extrapolate. Imagine. Read signs. Fill in blanks. Trust. It is impossible to know another human being completely, so the temptation when you love someone is to turn that person into who you want him to be, to project onto the other person what you imagine her to be. But part of true love, I think, is to let the other person remain a mystery, even as you work hard to see her clearly, to see him as he really is. The challenge of true love is to resist invention.

Don't draw what you think a chair looks like, the art teacher said in high school, *draw what you see when you look at the chair.*

Gordon Kaufman's God

The theologian is like an artist who constructs a picture of the world. But the theologian's finished product is not just something to hang on a wall. It is a work of art to be lived in.

We are here to love. We are here to give our lives not only to our neighbors, not only to our enemies, but to everyone and everything.

Devotion to God must humanize us—make us better, more loving, more just—and it must relativize us—guard against the tendency to make ourselves into gods.

We need to construct a new image of God. Scientific knowledge no longer allows the view of God as a man in the heavens who created the world. And massive outbreaks of evil and suffering have rendered the belief that human life is under the loving care of an all-powerful Father senseless.

I propose a new metaphor for God: serendipitous creativity—the coming into being of the previously nonexistent, the new, the novel.

True faith in God is not living with a conviction that everything is going to be okay in the end because we know God is taking care of us. True faith is acknowledging and accepting the ultimate mystery of things, but nevertheless moving forward creatively and with confidence—confidence in the serendipitous creativity that has brought us into being, that has sustained the human project within the web of life that surrounds and nurtures us, and that has given us a measure of hope for that project here on planet earth.

In 1945 an Egyptian farmer named Muhammad 'Ali al-Samman was digging for fertilizer in the hills near his home when he dug up new gospels, fourth-century papyrus books stuffed into a clay jar, most of them unknown before this unearthing. In the jar were fragmented copies of gospels—The Gospel of Thomas, The Gospel of Truth, The Gospel of Philip—and there were texts with titles like *The Thunder, Perfect Mind* and *The Apocryphon of John* and *The Hypostasis of*

the Archons and *The Exegesis of the Soul* and *The Apocalypse of Adam* and *The Sophia of Jesus Christ.*

I read these texts—now collected in the Nag Hammadi Library—in classes with Professor Karen King. In these manuscripts were sayings of Jesus I'd never heard before: "If those who lead you say to you, 'See the kingdom is in the sky,' then the birds of the sky will precede you. If they say to you, 'It is in the sea,' then the fish will precede you. Rather, the kingdom is inside of you, and it is outside of you." There were arguments that Jesus's teachings were more important than his death and resurrection. There were even stories that claimed the creator God I knew from Genesis was actually a wicked God who imprisoned the divine spark of humanity in mortal flesh. In some texts there was no God the Father, no hell, no eternal punishment, no wrath, and in other texts there were stories about leaders and disciples who were women. There were even feminine images of God.

People had believed in these buried texts. Some of them were written by women.

Not one book. Many books. Not four gospels, many gospels. An infinite number of stories to call holy. Studying them felt like reading a novel written collaboratively or like decoding a palimpsest. Endings crossed out and rewritten. Personalities changed. Accusations made. People killed off, then brought back to life. Story lines altered, taken apart, unwound, stitched back together again.

In the Gospel of Mary, Peter says to Mary, "Sister, we know that you were greatly loved by the Savior, as no other woman. Therefore tell us those words of the Savior which you know but which we haven't heard."

And Mary replies, "I will report to you as much as I remember that is unknown to you."

Even before I took King's class, I didn't believe the Bible was the literal word of God. I understood it to be a book written by human beings trying to make sense of God and of the world around them by telling stories, which was what I loved about the Bible—the metaphors, the parables, the four gospels instead of one. What I had not understood before King's class was that the book I called the Bible was a highly charged political document, the end product of hundreds of years of struggle over what should be included and what should be cut out. King taught me to ask this question every time I read a text: *What is at stake and for whom?* Like history, the Bible was put together by the victors in the battle over what counts as true. Heretic isn't a name you call yourself.

Every time I sit in a pew in a church on a Sunday morning, I'm asked to recite something, assent to something, acquiesce to some truth being offered to me. *Yes, Jesus is my personal savior. Yes, Jesus is the Son of God. Yes, Mary was a virgin. Yes, God has a plan even if we don't understand it. Yes, we believe in one God, Father the Almighty, Maker of heaven and earth. Yes, he will come again to judge the quick and the dead.* I often sense nostalgia, the longing for a simpler time when things were clearer, when people had real faith, were closer to the truth, when Jesus walked on the earth and people left everything they owned to follow him. But the history of Christianity is nothing like that. The further back you go the more complicated things get, the more diverse, the more confusing. No one agrees about anything. For everything I believe, there is someone else who has believed its opposite. Everything I call heresy was once called orthodoxy. Everything false was once also true.

Reading the texts that had been excised, buried, burned was like discovering that although I had always believed I was looking out a window at a landscape—at the real world—I was actually looking through a kaleidoscope with one eye closed. *But what if it looked like this?* King twisted one end, and the world fell into many colored fragments. *Or like this?* She twisted again, and new images appeared, fell to pieces, appeared, fell again, more beautiful than any scene I could have imagined. *We live our lives as if the way we think about the world is the way the world is*, she said. *How we think about things, then, makes all the difference.*

I have heard people compare Jesus to a person pointing to the moon—the moon is God and Jesus's finger pointing to it is Christianity. *We have mistaken the finger pointing to the moon for the moon itself,* they say. But in divinity school I learned my vision had been narrower than that. I hadn't even seen the finger. I had been bending over a microscope looking at skin cells scraped from someone's knuckle and pressed between two pieces of glass. *Look*, I had been saying. *The moon.*

Throughout my childhood, I struggled to make sense of the doctrine I was fed on Sundays. I tried to follow the pattern set by the institutional church, to mold myself into someone else's shape, to be the girl I was told God wanted me to be. At All Saints the pattern shifted to include a God who loved me and was committed to justice in the world, and then the classes I took in divinity school threw Christianity wide open. Christianity was not about single truths but about multiplicity, translations, silences, arguments, new voices. Asking questions, disagreeing and doubting were essential parts of faith, not anathemas to it. I was ready to stand and take my place in a long line of critics. There was room for me.

. . .

And there was room for my rage. What had been removed, what had been written in, what had been written out—none of it was accidental.

Christianity has long been manipulated to make domination seem natural, inevitable, part of the divine plan, blessed. It has been used to sanction anything human beings want to do to one another. War. Sexism. Bigotry. Heterosexism. Racism. Segregation. Torture. For centuries, slave owners insisted the Bible supported slavery. Why else would it tell slaves to obey their masters? Slavery must be in line with God's will, they argued, part of the natural order, a result of the curse of Ham—and if slavery is in line with God's will, then it can't be morally wrong, they insisted, it has to be morally right. Inequality became divinely ordained and equality became a sin. And after slavery, racism was supported by white Christianity. Some ministers joined the KKK. They cancelled church and rented buses so their congregations could attend lynchings on Sunday mornings—so they could share picnic lunches and watch black men and women be tortured, burned, mutilated, hung from trees, and murdered, so they could take photographs of this violence and send the images to their friends.

Just because something ended up in a book called the Bible doesn't make it right.

One of my professors, Elisabeth Schüssler Fiorenza, taught me to read against interpretations of the Bible that render women invisible. Women were there—standing in crowds next to Jesus, included as part of the disciples, acting as priests—even if sexist language hides their presence, she said. Find the word "men" in the biblical text, for example. Ask why the translators chose the word "men" instead of "people." Many will tell you the translators used the word "men" because it is an inclusive term: *Don't worry! 'Men' includes women, silly girl!* But if you then ask why women can't get ordained, they will point to the same word and tell you women can't be ordained because Jesus was a man and all his disciples were men.

I can't help it, people say when institutional sexism is brought to their attention. They shrug their shoulders. They throw up their hands. *I didn't make it up. It's right there in the Bible.*

We know God isn't a man, the priests say, but then they lead their congregations in Our Father.

Tertullian defines women as the devil's gateway and Augustine insists women are not made in the image of God and Aquinas classifies women as misbegotten males and Luther argues God created Adam to lord over all living creatures until Eve ruined everything. "Women have had the power of *naming* stolen from us," Mary Daly writes in *Beyond God the Father.* "We have not been free to use our own power to name ourselves, the world, or God . . . To exist humanly is to name the self, the world, and God . . . a reclaiming of the right to name."

Elizabeth Cady Stanton, a nineteenth-century proponent of women's rights, insisted women needed to read the Bible critically because passages from the text were used as proof of the holiness of women's oppression. She formed a committee of women to create *The Woman's Bible*. They read from Genesis to Revelation and marked all the texts that concerned women. They then cut out those marked passages, pasted them into blank books, and wrote their own commentaries underneath. "For all the religions on the face of the earth degrade [woman]," she writes. "And so long as woman accepts the position that they assign her, emancipation is impossible."

How others see God—what they call God, how they define God, the language they use to talk about God—affects how they see you. And how you see God—what you call God, how you define God, the language you use to talk about God—affects not only how you see others but also how you see yourself. What does it do to call God "Father"? "Lord"? "King"? What does it do to imagine God as a man? What does it do to a little girl to grow up being told she is not made in the image of God? What does it do to tell her she cannot be a priest because she is a girl? How would things be different if God were imagined as a woman?

Many of my professors were feminists, my friends were feminists, the chaplain at the divinity school was a feminist, the ordained ministers I knew at school were feminists, and I wasn't going to church anywhere other than the weekly Wednesday noon worship at school, so being a feminist theologian felt completely compatible with being a Christian. An essential component of the Christian theological project has always been to criticize old versions of God and to construct new ones, and I believed I was taking up my part of this traditional work.

I hadn't yet admitted that sexism was woven into the very fabric of Christianity, that to pull on that thread would mean the whole enterprise would unravel. So, at first, my feminist work didn't challenge in any fundamental way my belief in God. I had the sense that I was peeling back layers of racism and misogyny, peeling back mistakes, misunderstandings, mistranslations, and that deep down, at the center, at the core, I would find that God was good, and with enough careful, critical intellectual work, I would be able to claim a true, real, authentic version of God, and I would be able to believe in it—and so would everyone else.

I was sure I knew the real God. I was like the wife who convinces herself she's the only one who truly knows her husband. All that other stuff—the drinking, the sleeping around, the bravado, the lies—that's not who he is. That's who other people think he is, but they don't understand him because they can't really see him. They mistake him for the jerks he spends time with. They don't know what he's like when it's just the two of us, when we're alone and he's sweet and kind and loving. They don't hear him tell me I'm the only one who understands him, that I can never leave or he won't survive, that it's the two of us against the world.

Mary Daly's God

Go back to the beginning, back to the garden, to the sleeping Adam and the rib removed, to the man who gives birth to his wife, to the serpent and the woman and the fruit of the tree, to the curse of an angry God and the punishment of painful childbirth and desire for a husband who will rule over her, to the promise of sweat and bread and returning to dust, to blaming woman for the fall of the world. Tell a different story.

It's time to leave the Looking Glass society, where women function as mirrors that reflect men at twice their actual size. Time to go beyond God the Father. Don't you see? If God is male, then the male is God.

Reclaim the right to name your self, your world, your God. The liberation of language is rooted in the liberation of ourselves. Be a wild woman. Shift the shapes of words, of worlds. Why must God be a noun? Why not a verb? God is not A Being. God is Be-ing.

They will call you a witch, the devil's gateway, a misbegotten male. They will call you a sinner. *Lower your voices,* they'll say. *Have some humility. Be patient. All in God's time.* They will ask, *Who do you think you are?*

And you will answer: I am not a stranger, an outsider. I am daughter. Weaver. Messenger. Courageous, Outrageous,

Furious. Moon-Wise Spell-Caster. And I am journeying beyond.

As a student in the master of divinity program, I was required to complete two units of field education, a real-life experience designed to help me learn the skills I would need to become a minister. Most students worked in homeless shelters or churches or after-school programs or hospitals or prisons, but one of my friends at school was a poet named Katie Ford, and she heard it was possible to design your own field education project, something called a student-initiated project. If the Office of Ministry Studies agreed to support your independent project, they would act as your field education site and would pay you a stipend. "What if we proposed a joint project?" she asked. "I could write poems and you could paint."

I was sure we'd get laughed right out of the Office of Ministry Studies, but we wrote a proposal anyway and met with the head of the field education program and explained what we wanted to do—Katie would write poems, I would create paintings in response to her words, and we would have an exhibit of our work the following fall in the school's chapel. He was quiet while he read our proposal. Katie and I looked at each other across the room, lifted our eyebrows. I was sweating. He raised his head. "That's a fantastic idea," he said.

We left his office and grabbed onto each other and made our way out of the two heavy doors to the front lawn, where we jumped up and down. We'd convinced Harvard to give us money to spend the summer making art.

At the end of Raymond Carver's story "Cathedral," the narrator and a friend of the narrator's wife—a man who is blind—sit together in the narrator's living room. His wife is asleep, and the television is on, a show about the church and the Middle Ages. The narrator watches the television screen. The blind man listens. Then a cathedral appears on the screen, and the narrator, realizing the blind man has never seen a cathedral, asks him if he has any idea what a cathedral is. *I know they took hundreds of workers fifty or a hundred years to build*, the blind man says. *The men who began their life's work on them, they never lived to see the completion of their work.* The blind man asks the narrator to describe a cathedral. The narrator tries, using words like *tall* and *sky* and *stone.* Then the blind man has an idea. He asks the narrator to get a pen and some heavy paper. The blind man closes his hand over the narrator's hand, which is holding the pen. *Draw,* he says. *I'll follow along with you.* And the narrator begins to draw, first a box that looks like a house, then spires, windows, arches, flying buttresses. The blind man says, *Close your eyes now,* and the narrator closes his eyes, and they keep drawing together. *His fingers rode my fingers as my hand went over the paper. It was like nothing else in my life up to now.*

. . .

Because I'd moved from a big apartment near Fresh Pond to a tiny apartment closer to the divinity school—a space so small that the landlord had to cut a rectangle out of the bathroom door so it could close around the toilet—I needed a studio, a place to paint. I knew another student at school who was an artist and had a studio, so I called to ask if there might be room available in the building where he worked. He gave me the phone number for the Washington Street Art Center, and within a month, I had a space there.

The Washington Street Art Center backed up to train tracks and had been a bus depot before it housed artists' studios. Other artists were always working when I was there, painters and photographers and sculptors, and there was usually music: Radiohead, PJ Harvey, Nina Simone. I spent every day in my studio that summer. Katie wrote poems and delivered them to me when we met for coffee each week. I taped her words into my sketchbook. I read them again and again, and then I sat on a stool in my studio with the light coming in all around and closed my eyes. I drew images in colored pencil on the big white pages of my sketchbook, and I put paint on canvas—bright colors, lines, thick layers of paint. Painting quieted the voices in my mind, even my Censor. In the studio my mind was still. *Blue blue blue blue blue,* I thought. *Yellow yellow yellow yellow yellow.*

I imagined God in my studio, in the butterfly chair in the corner of my space reading passages chosen from the lost and buried holy texts to remind me I was participating in the ongoing work of creation. *Listen to this,* God said. *'If you bring forth what is within you, what you bring forth will save you. If you do not bring forth what is in you, what you do not bring forth will destroy you.'*

. . .

I didn't have a car, so every two weeks I took the bus to Brookline and walked a few blocks and then up to a house at the top of a steep hill to meet with Martina, my therapist. I went around to the back of the house, followed a stone-lined path through leafy plants, ducked under some latticework, opened the small door to the basement, and climbed four flights of narrow stairs.

Martina told me about a kind of therapy called Eye Movement Desensitization and Reprocessing, or EMDR: I would describe an event in my life that was disturbing to me, something I still experienced as traumatic. I would tell Martina the feeling I had when

I thought of that experience, and then I would describe how I would like to feel instead.

Martina brought her chair to the end of the couch so we faced each other, our knees side by side. "Think of that disturbing image," she said, and then she moved her hand back and forth in front of my face. I tracked her hand movements with my eyes, without moving my head, as if following the swinging watch of a hypnotist, and while I moved my eyes, images went through my mind. At regular intervals, she stopped moving her hand and asked, "What do you see?" And I described what I saw in my imagination, and she wrote down what I said on a yellow legal pad, and then she moved her hand back and forth in front of my eyes again. Doing EMDR was like dreaming while awake.

During every EMDR session, I spent twenty minutes of my ninety-minute session coming up with the disturbing feeling and the replacement feeling—even though they were always the same. Martina was patient. "How do you feel when you think of that scene?" she asked.

"I don't know," I said. "I'm not sure."

She waited while I tried to figure it out, even though I imagine she knew I would say the same thing I had said the week before and the week before that and the week before that: *I feel like I have done something wrong. I feel like I am unlovable.*

"What do you want to feel?" Martina asked.

"I am good. I am lovable," I would finally say, and then we could begin:

Think of that scene. Follow my hand.

Now what do you see?

I am a child in a crib. I am on fire. I am screaming for help and no one comes to get me. A man walks by the crib and sprinkles me with holy water. Just before the flames consume me I remember my heart is a fountain. I turn it on and put the flames out myself.

Good. Follow my hand.

Now what do you see?

I am trapped in a giant birdcage with another woman. I realize the door is unlocked. I walk out and tell her to follow me, tell her we are free. She stays in the cage. *How can you abandon me? You ungrateful brat!* she screams, but I keep walking, stuffing my ears with cotton. I don't look back.

Good. Follow my hand.

Now what do you see?

I am standing in a kitchen, and I am visited by an angel. *Here,* the angel says, *this is for you.* She hands me a heart-shaped image, a picture of me as a little girl, curled up and cradled in the hand of God. *Put this heart in your pocket,* the angel says. *Plug your heart into this heart, and you will never run out of love.* I do what she tells me to do. I plug my heart into the God-heart I carry in my pocket. Light pours out of me. Wings open out of my back.

"Now how true do the words *I have done something wrong. I am unlovable* feel?" Martina asked.

"Not true at all."

"How true do the words *I am good. I am lovable* feel?"

"They feel irrelevant, too small." I said. "Because I'm love."

. . .

Later that summer, Katie handed me a poem:

Soon my eyes will adjust so that what I know is true is also what I see.
Revelation always works this way: Metaphor first, then the healing.

A Philosopher's God

God does not create the world, Alfred North Whitehead writes, God saves it: or, more accurately, God is the poet of the world, with patience leading it by his vision of truth, beauty, and goodness. God shows us what is possible, pours back into the world what is worth saving. I offer you this image: God is best conceived as a tender care that nothing is lost.

The theological possibilities I discovered in school renewed my desire to be a priest. I wanted to share what I had learned with a community—to show the kind of expansive thinking about God that was possible, to illustrate how God language could change the world, to work together to do good. I thought other people would be as excited about these new ways of thinking as I was. Theology was a construction, but that didn't mean that God wasn't real. It meant that God was God. That anything was possible. That we could create the version of God we needed to save the world. I remembered Ann Ulanov's lecture I'd heard at Yale: Dip brushes in color. Paint something new. Believe God can take it.

I convinced myself I could keep it all together, that God was big enough to include all the versions of God competing for my devotion. Serendipitous creativity. Feminist theology. The God who loved me through the night. But the strain was starting to show.

After returning from a trip to Texas and carrying an enormous suitcase up the three flights of stairs to my tiny apartment, I found myself awake and in searing pain in the dead of night. In the emergency room I learned I had ruptured a disc in my back—L4/5, my lumbar spine—a disc that was now pressing into my spinal cord. I couldn't lift my left foot all the way, so I spent the rest of the semester falling down on the uneven brick sidewalks of Cambridge, which made me, eventually, agree to back surgery.

Soon after that, doctors found yet another irregular mole on my skin. I'd had several moles removed before that one—all benign—but this one came back atypical: *dysplastic nevus,* the kind of mole that can eventually become melanoma. Katie had written a poem about being allergic to bees, and a line from that poem came to mind while I listened to the doctor explain she needed to cut my skin again to get clean margins: *What am I made of that I could be killed by such a small thing*?

And soon after that, doctors found two polyps in my colon—the kind that eventually can develop into colon cancer. The polyps, like the disc, like the moles, were cut out.

My body knew. Pieces were leaving me.

I was seeing an acupuncturist for the pain in my back. "Are you grieving?" he asked.

"No," I said. "I don't think so."

"Your body is showing all the signs of grief," he said and then explained that in Chinese medicine, grief and sadness are associated with the lungs.

"I'm not grieving," I said, and started to cry. I struggled to breathe.

Things would not hold. My body knew.

. . .

I had applied to the doctoral program in theology at Harvard, but I hadn't been accepted. So, once again, I found myself at the end of something with no idea what to do next. During all three years of divinity school I told people I was studying to be a priest, but the only thing I had done to move toward ordination was to take a preaching class with John Spong, the retired bishop of the Episcopal Diocese in Newark, a leader in the fight for equal rights for LGBT people in the Episcopal Church. I loved preaching, and I was good at it. I won the school's annual preaching contest. I was invited to give the sermon at a Communion service celebrated by Archbishop Desmond Tutu. I was chosen as the student speaker for commencement.

One of the requirements for ordination in the Episcopal Church is that you need to belong to an Episcopal church, a basic expectation, obvious, but I still didn't count myself a member of any church. I didn't even go to church. Just thinking about waking up early on Sunday mornings, sitting in an uncomfortable pew, listening to mediocre sermons, reciting creeds, and calling God "Father" made my chest get tight.

I fooled myself into thinking it was no big deal that I preferred to do almost anything on Sunday mornings other than going to church. Cleaning my bathroom. Reorganizing my closet. Arriving at the library right when it opened. I imagined my Sunday morning absences didn't bother God at all. I imagined he never said anything when he dragged himself out of our warm bed early on Sunday mornings to go pray and sing and be worshipped. I imagined he always kissed me before he left and made sure the coffee would still be warm by the time I got out of bed and was ready to drink it. But if God really loved me, my failure to find a church should have worried him. He should have wondered how serious I could possibly be about our future together. He should have doubted my faith in him and questioned whether our love affair had been site specific, whether it could survive three thousand miles from the city of angels and the community I'd found at All Saints.

But if my Sunday mornings did concern God, he never let on. He gave me space to do what I needed to do, to explore what I needed to explore, to try what I needed to try. That's what I loved about him. How gentle he was during that time, how supportive, how accepting. But that's also what I grew to hate about him. His hands-off approach to everything. His refusal to do anything too dramatic or overly emotional or outright salvific. His silence. He was just so stubbornly passive. When I stopped going to church, he didn't do a single thing about it. He never said he missed me. He didn't fight for himself. Or for us. He had to know how things were going to turn out, but he just sat there, watching me put down the letters that would eventually spell the end of our story together, doing nothing to try to make things turn out differently.

. . .

By the end of divinity school, it was no longer possible to ignore the crevasse that had opened between my intellectual version of God and my personal version of God, but I believed I could bridge the gap. I came up with a plan: I needed a job, and I needed to belong to a church to get ordained, so I would get a job at an Episcopal Church. Feed two birds with one seed. I took a temporary job in the Office of Ministry Studies at Harvard working at the front desk and answering phones, and I applied for jobs in churches.

But while I wrote cover letters and worked on my résumé and asked for letters of recommendation, I knew I didn't really want any of the jobs for which I was applying. I knew I was throwing myself at a man I didn't desire anymore simply because I'd spent so much time imagining he was right for me, because I'd invested so much energy making myself right for him.

. . .

During my last week at the Office of Ministry Studies, I was in the basement of the divinity school making copies when a woman walked by and said, "Did you hear? A small plane flew into the World Trade Center in New York City."

"What?" I asked.

"It must have been an accident," she said, and I pictured a pilot in a tiny propeller plane making a mistake and flying into a building. I leaned against the warm machine and finished making copies. I went upstairs and sat at my desk.

Someone turned on the radio in the office. I listened to voices. A plane flew into the World Trade Center. Another plane flew into the World Trade Center. A plane flew into the Pentagon. And there was a missing plane. How do you lose a plane? People around me talked about the possibility that our military might shoot that plane out of the sky. What it would mean if our government gave orders to shoot down a plane filled with people?

I went home and watched the events I had heard on the radio happen on television. Watched the second plane hit, the first building fall, the second building fall, again, again.

Later I heard someone found a pelvic bone on the roof of his apartment building in New York City. *The pelvic bone is like a bowl,* my yoga teacher says. *Tilt the bowl and let what you carry flow out.* When I hear the words "September 11" now, I think of that bone on the roof and what has to happen to a body for a bone to be all that's left.

5

WHO ARE YOU AND WHY ARE YOU IN MY HOUSE?

I KNEW RIGHT AWAY things weren't going to go well for me at the suburban church outside Boston. I knew it during the interview for the job, knew it when the rector brought me into the sanctuary and we stood in front of the pulpit and she said that the preacher's job is to be Christ's presence for the flock, and I nodded even though that isn't how I think about preaching at all. I knew it when I saw the Stations of the Cross lined up along one wall of the sanctuary—Jesus carrying the cross, Jesus being whipped, Jesus hanging from the cross, Jesus dead in his mother's arms—and all I could think when I looked at those images was that the shirtless men standing around holding flimsy whips and chains and wearing mini-toga-skirts and sandals looked like they were in a low-budget porno.

I knew it wouldn't work, but I wanted it to work. I needed it to. I needed a job. I needed to know what I was doing with my life. I needed to keep telling people I was going to be a priest. So I took the job as the church school coordinator and the youth minister and agreed with theology I didn't believe in and tried to be good, tried to get people at the church to like me. I was clever and faithful. I baked cookies with the congregants' children. I ordered pizza for the youth group. I translated all the things I heard about God at church into words I could agree with, and I translated all the things I believed about God into words people at the church might agree with. I metaphorized. I improvised. I bent. I crammed myself into the small spaces allowed for me in the liturgy, in between the pews, under the altar.

Until I didn't. Until I couldn't.

. . .

"People are upset about your sermons," the rector of the church said, sitting on the other side of a giant shiny brown desk covered with a layer of glass so nothing could nick its surface. I hadn't been working at the church for very long. I'd just preached my second sermon.

"Which people?" I asked.

"A lot of people," she said.

"They haven't spoken to me," I said.

"Of course they haven't," she said.

"How many people?"

"It's hard to say," she said.

I waited.

"Three," she said.

The week before, the United States accidentally bombed a Red Cross building in Afghanistan. Ground Zero was still burning. *What if the burning buildings—the Red Cross tent and the smoldering abyss that was once the Twin Towers—are a contemporary burning bush?* I asked in my sermon. *What if God, from the flames, is calling us toward peace?*

"Have you noticed that you use a lot of fire imagery?" she asked. "Something's always burning in your sermons. Try to avoid flame metaphors next time."

"Is that the main complaint people have about my preaching?" I asked. "Flames?"

"No," she said. "They want you to talk more about Jesus."

I could have talked more about Jesus, but I didn't think many people in the church would want to hear what I had to say. My Jesus was a version of the liberation theology Jesus, a revolutionary, an activist executed for standing up to the state, for standing up for the poor, for speaking truth to power—and although I knew other people in the congregation also embraced this version of Jesus, it was not the Jesus worshipped by the people complaining about my sermons. They wanted me to talk about a different Jesus. The Jesus who requires nothing from you but belief—the Jesus who was the only son of God, the Jesus who rose from the dead. The John 3:16 Jesus.

Their complaint, I soon learned, was a kind of code: talk more about faith and less about politics. But faith and politics weren't separate for me, which was the very reason I wanted to get ordained. I went to divinity school after teaching in Compton because I thought churches could help make the world more just and life-giving for everyone, and what I learned at school had confirmed my belief that God—or a particular version of God—could help bring a better world into being. God had become part of politics for me—a symbol that could spur liberation or oppression, a symbol that could do great good or terrible harm.

This was not a particularly quiet time for Christianity in the United States. George W. Bush was president and was waging two wars—one in Afghanistan and one in Iraq—with the justifications for this violence wrapped in Christian rhetoric. I marched against both wars, but despite the fact that these were some of the largest worldwide protests ever, the United States and its allies invaded both countries.

This was also when Gene Robinson was elected bishop of the Episcopal Diocese in New Hampshire, the first openly gay bishop. His election and consecration made more visible the anti-gay hatred in the church and initiated yet another discussion about gay rights. *Should gay people be ordained? Should the church perform gay marriages? Is homosexuality an abomination?* To answer these questions, opponents of Gene Robinson turned to the Bible—Leviticus, the letters from Paul. *The Bible says, the Bible says, the Bible says,* they chanted again and again, and all I wanted to say was, *God doesn't speak English.* Their anxious prooftexting seemed absurd to me. *You're taking the Bible literally?* I thought. *You can't be serious!*

But they were serious, and even more troubling to me were the other people in the church—even those in support of equal rights for everyone—who were taking the Bible quoters seriously, taking their bigotry seriously, their pick-and-choose textual analysis seriously. They were entertaining homophobia as a viable—even a possibly blessed—position. *There are faithful people on both sides of the debate,* was the refrain both in my particular church and in the Episcopal Church at large.

What's faithful about hate?

When same-sex marriage was made legal in Massachusetts, I went to Cambridge City Hall at midnight and watched the couples line up, watched them walk through the door to get their marriage licenses, watched them walk back out with their hands in the air cheering, rings and tears, roses, champagne, balloons, streamers. Police were there, too—there to protect us from the people on the other side of the street holding an enormous sign that said "God Hates Fags."

Many of the people against the full inclusion of LGBT folks are also against the ordination of women. And the fact that Christian homophobia and misogyny are linked—that they depend on the same logic, use the same strategies—scared me, a woman seeking ordination in a church with some dioceses, even whole countries, that still didn't ordain women. Gene Robinson had to wear a bulletproof vest to his consecration ceremony. People wanted to *kill* him. The rector of the church where I worked was a woman—a position that is still rare for women to hold, especially in big, thriving churches like that one—and during my first meeting with her, she pointed to a large gray rock sitting on top of a pile of papers and asked, "Do you see this rock?"

"Yes," I said.

"It looks like a paperweight, doesn't it? But I have it here within reach in case I need to use it to protect myself," she said. "You should do the same." She then told me how frightening it is to be a woman in the church, not just at night when a stranger might wander into the empty building off the street, but all the time, every day.

I wasn't supposed to talk about any of this in church—not gay marriage, not the ordination of Gene Robinson, not the wars, not sexism. I was told there was a variety of opinions in the church, and that I was called to minister to everyone, not just to the people with whom I happened to agree.

The priest at my friend's church spent the day visiting people at a hospital. Hospital policy was that clergy didn't have to pay for parking, so on the way out of the parking lot she handed the attendant her ticket on which she had written her name and the name of her church. He looked at the ticket and then looked back at her. She was wearing her clerical collar. "I go to a Bible-believing church," the attendant said.

"Yes?" the priest said.

"There aren't any women priests in the Bible," he said.

"There aren't any cars in the Bible either," she said.

He lifted the gate.

A Theologian's God

Whatever concerns you ultimately becomes god for you, Paul Tillich writes. Everything is open to consecration.

There are several misconceptions about faith. The most ordinary is to think of faith as knowledge with little evidence, but this is "belief," not "faith." Another is to think of faith as believing something that someone with authority tells you. This, too, is a mistake. Faith isn't about taking someone else's word for something. Faith is about participating in the subject of your ultimate concern with your whole being.

Having faith in your ultimate concern is the greatest risk you can take. If it proves to be a failure, if you discover you have surrendered yourself to something that was not worth it, then the meaning of your life breaks down. You will find you have given away your center without a chance to regain it.

While I understood "God" to be the most powerful word in the English language—so powerful that using it felt like picking up a weapon, unwieldy, dangerous—people at church used the word casually, seemingly without careful attention, or else they didn't use it at all. Each week we followed the liturgy set out in the *Book of Common Prayer.* We preached on the lectionary texts. We chose hymns out of the hymnal. We recited creeds and formulaic prayers. And that was that.

In our weekly staff meetings we barely talked about God. Theology, it seemed, was not the point of running a church. Being an institution was the point. Raising money, obeying the hierarchy, following rules, being right, counting the number of people in the pews, deciding whether or not to expand the building or get a new roof, caring for the community—that was church work. And I'm not sure many people in the congregation came to church to talk about God, either. They came to church because they wanted to be in a community with one another. They came to figure out how to live a life with meaning, how to do good work in the world, how to give back, how to be better people. They came to church to be fed, with bread and wine during Communion. They craved connection, and church seemed like a place where this might happen. God was almost incidental to the whole enterprise—background noise.

Although I focused a lot of energy on those who complained about my sermons, most people liked my sermons and the rest simply ignored them. If you had asked people in the congregation what they believed, I doubt their beliefs would have mapped onto the Nicene Creed any more closely than mine would have. And like me, they probably didn't completely believe in the version of God described each week in the liturgy or in the prayers. They were very faithful people, but their faith had little to do with theology and much more to do with the other people sitting next to them in the pews and kneeling next to them at the Communion rail week after week. They came to church to be with each other, and they happened to come to that particular church because they'd been raised Episcopalian or their spouse had been raised Episcopalian or they had friends who also attended that church or the church was close to where they lived. I suspect most were willing to overlook sexist language or dangerous theology because they hadn't expected to hear anything different.

But I couldn't overlook it.

I was deeply disappointed. The distance between the theology I studied in school and the theology being practiced in the pews and preached from the pulpit by the priests on staff was enormous. Everything I took for granted—the difference between "God" and God, the wide range of theological possibilities, the need to think critically about the effects God-talk can have on the world, the existence of other holy texts besides those collected in the Bible, historical criticism—was absent, even heretical. I felt like I was going crazy. The God I had come to believe in was nowhere to be found—and in that God's place was a different version of God I struggled to recognize. I felt as if there had been an invasion of the body snatchers, or as if I had traveled backward in time, before feminist or liberation or queer or black theology. The vision of God being worshipped in that place was so narrow. *What is going on?* I wanted to shout.

I sometimes wonder how doctors, having seen inside the human body, having dissected it, go about their daily lives interacting with the rest of us. When they look at people, do they see what is happening on the inside? The map of veins and arteries? The liver, the spleen, the stomach? Do they think of the skeleton? The skull? Do they think of the limbs they've cut off or the cancer they've cut out?

Divinity school had been like an autopsy of my faith. I had peeled back the layers of skin, of fat and muscle. I had looked inside to see how it worked, held its heart in my hand, touched its bones, its lungs. And it didn't look the same anymore. Nothing looked the same.

I heard a story on the radio about a woman who came home from work and sat next to a man who was waiting for her on her front porch. He was wearing her husband's clothes. "Who are you?" the woman asked.

"Who are you?" he said, laughing. "Come over here and give me a kiss."

She gave him a kiss, but it felt wrong. *His essence, his soul, isn't in there,* she thought. *He's an impostor.*

Capgras syndrome—the feeling that the person you love has been replaced by an impostor.

Some scientists explain Capgras syndrome as a kind of denial—there are parts of the person you love that you don't like, and when you see those negative parts you say, *He must be a different person.* People can show you fingerprints. They can show you photographs. They can map his genetic code. They can give you all kinds of proof, but you will not believe them. The only way to cope with the recognition that the person you love is not the person you thought he was, is to say, *This is not the person I know. This is an impostor.* The only thing to do is make a break.

Other scientists explain Capgras syndrome by looking at the brain: When you see the person you love, the visual parts of the brain recognize that person and send the message, *That is my husband* to the amygdala, the part of the brain that stores our emotional memories. Your husband is both a face you recognize and a set of feelings that goes with his face. But if you have a head injury, if there is something wrong with your brain, if the wire connecting the visual part of the brain to the emotional part of the brain has been cut, then he will look like your husband, but you won't have the feelings you associate with your husband. No husband feelings: *impostor.*

Who are you? I ask God.

Who are you? God says. *Come over here and give me a kiss.*

. . .

Soon after the start of the war in Iraq, I went to the gym. I belonged to a women's gym in Porter Square, and sometimes when I was exhausted, I went there just to sit in the hot tub. "Have a great workout," one of the friendly women at the front desk would say, and I would feel morally obligated to admit why I was there. "I'm not working out," I would say. "I'm just going to sit in the hot tub."

I sunk into the deep water. I hadn't been sleeping well. I hated my job at the church. Some of my friends had been arrested during anti-war protests. All the marching I'd done hadn't made any difference. People were dying. I soaked for a long time—much longer than the posted warning signs suggested I should—and then I climbed out of the hot tub, reached for my towel that was hanging on a hook, and fainted head-first down a flight of white tile steps. When I woke up, I was on my back on the floor, naked, blood running down my face, two kind strangers kneeling over me.

They'd seen me fall and were more distraught than I was.

"It's going to be all right," one of the women said. "An ambulance is on the way."

"Could I please have a towel?" I kept asking, but no one seemed to be able to hear me over the commotion I had caused in the locker room and the shower area. Right before the paramedics arrived, someone covered me with a robe.

"You got here fast," I said to one of the men in dark blue uniforms loading me onto a gurney.

"We heard 'women's gym' and 'hot tub' and got here as quickly as we could," he said.

They drove me to the hospital in an ambulance. The wound in the middle of my forehead was shaped like a lightning bolt, and in the curtained room the doctor told me I didn't need stitches, and then he glued my head back together.

. . .

I had entered the ordination process almost as soon as I started working at the church. I told the rector I might like to get ordained, and the next thing I knew I was meeting her early on a Saturday morning in front of the diocesan offices for the first official meeting for all people beginning the process. At the meeting, she ushered me around the room, introducing me to key players, whispering helpful hints in my ear. At lunch she maneuvered me over to the circle of folding chairs where the bishop was sitting. We sat right next to him. "Tom," she said. "This is the woman I was telling you about."

The rector put together a discernment committee for me at the church, a group of people charged with the task of determining whether or not I was called to be a priest, the first step of the ordination process. I met with my committee every month in a room down the hall from my office. They asked me questions about my faith, my family, my reasons for wanting to be a priest. I knew there were right answers to their questions—"When they ask you why you want to be a priest, tell them it's because you want to celebrate the Eucharist," the rector said—but the official answers didn't match my honest answers. I decided to tell the truth in those meetings. I talked about theology as imaginative construction, about Jesus as an activist, about my understanding that if God was present in Jesus, then God could be present in each of us. I talked about my frustration with sexist language and theology. And my committee supported my views, even when they didn't agree with them.

Before I bought a car, I borrowed friends' cars to drive to the church, cars with bumper stickers that said things like "God Is Coming and Is She Pissed," or "Militant Agonistic: I don't know and you don't either,"or "If you're against abortion, don't have one." When I finally bought a car, a used green Volkswagen Golf, I put my own bumper sticker on it, a gift from a friend: "STOP THIS SEXIST SHIT."

And no one at the church seemed to mind.

But I wanted them to mind. I was looking for a fight.

I heard a voice whispering, *I don't want to be a priest*, but I believed I was too far in to quit. I had completed a three-year degree designed to prepare people for ministry. I had reapplied and been admitted to a doctoral program in theology. I was working at a church. I was going through the ordination process. What in the world would I do if I didn't do this?

I don't want to be a priest.

I've walked too far down this path to turn around.

I don't want to be a priest.

I'm not a quitter.

I don't want to be a priest.

Late one night, alone in my apartment, I took the Belief-O-Matic™ test on Beliefnet.com just to see what I might find out, to see if it might have some wisdom for me. "Even if YOU don't know what faith you are, Belief-O-Matic™ knows," the website promised. So I answered twenty questions about my concept of God, the afterlife, human nature, the problem of evil, the reasons for suffering, the importance of nonviolence and social justice, and when the results appeared on the screen, I was "100 percent Quaker." Then Jewish. Then Unitarian Universalist. Then Buddhist. Mainline Protestant didn't even make the top ten.

When I was living in L.A. and teaching in Compton, Maylen moved to L.A. from New York City with her new boyfriend, Phil. They met when they were both studying for the MCAT and applying to medical school, and they had been together for less than six months when they realized they didn't want to be doctors and packed Phil's 1986 Lincoln Continental and drove to Los Angeles and moved into an apartment together right on the beach.

"Every fight we had that first year we lived together was basically the same fight," Maylen said. "They might have sounded different on the surface, but underneath we were asking the same question: Who are you and why are you in my house?"

Whose house was I in?

I didn't want to withdraw from the ordination process. I wanted to be kicked out. That would confirm my biggest fear—that I had done something wrong, that I was unlovable—and it would also allow me to avoid the truth: I didn't want to be a priest anymore. It was over.

I wanted to be able to say to God, *It's not you, it's me*, but I was afraid *It's not me, it's you* was closer to the truth. How do you end a relationship with God? How do you leave the most powerful being in the universe? And if you do, if you're brave enough to walk out of that house and close the door behind you, where do you go? What story do you tell?

Admitting being a priest was not what I wanted to do with my life—admitting the vocation did not fit me anymore, that it may have never fit—was terrifying. It was easier to keep throwing myself against a closed door than to turn around and see the open door right behind me. It was easier to blame everyone else for my misery. To think other people were idiots. I had invested years of my life in something I desperately wanted to want to do. Because it sounded good. Because it would please other people. Because it would make me special. Holy. Good. Because I needed the look in other people's eyes when I said I was going to be a priest. Because I longed for the comfort that came in the dark of night, the brief relief from the shame that followed me around. What I wanted more than anything was to be loved unconditionally, and I had been willing to do anything to get that feeling. Who better to fill the endless emptiness inside me than God?

If people at church would tell me I wasn't called to be a priest, then I wouldn't have to admit it to myself. It was easier to focus on other things—the man in the congregation who walked around during coffee hour and asked women if they had seen the *Vagina Monologues* just so he could say the word vagina, the sexist language of the liturgy, the rector's criticism of what I wore ("Is it bag lady day today?"), the people who complained about my sermons.

From the outside, the gymnasium at Yale looks like a cathedral. The story goes that the woman who donated the money for the building really donated the money for a cathedral, but Yale needed a gym, not a cathedral, so they made the building look like a cathedral and then drove her by the building to show it to her. She loved it so much, people say, that she never asked to see the inside of the building, never knew it was all squash and basketball and swimming.

I was like Yale's gym. I looked like a Christian, like a person preparing to be a priest, but I was something else on the inside altogether.

. . .

A seven-year-old girl at the church where I worked was diagnosed with a brain tumor. That summer I taught vacation bible school, and she and her younger brother came to my class together. One morning, I gave everyone a disposable camera, and we went into the garden to take pictures of things we were thankful for. At the end of the day I sent them home with their cameras to take more gratitude photographs there. She was too sick to come to vacation Bible school after that, but her brother brought me her camera a few weeks later, and before I made time to get her photographs developed, she died. *God must have needed another little angel in heaven*, I heard someone say to the girl's mother in the church basement after her memorial service while we watched a slideshow of family photographs.

Around the same time, my friend Chantal's fiancé, Charlie, was diagnosed with stomach cancer. He was twenty-eight. Chantal and Charlie got married on a bluff overlooking the Pacific Ocean, and Charlie died before he turned thirty. People Chantal barely knew tried to comfort her by saying things like, *Charlie's in a better place now* or *God has reasons we don't understand* or *Things happen for a reason.*

I spoke at Charlie's memorial service, standing in the center of a circle of trees, grapevines in fields all around. I didn't mention God at all, but one woman found me after the service, and her rage about his death was visible, about to break through her skin. She knew I was going through the ordination process and was studying to be a priest. "Tell me about this God of yours, Sarah," she said, gripping my arm, and I didn't know if she needed me to believe in God or if she would slap me if I did.

We drove back to Charlie and Chantal's house after the service and gathered in their backyard, where there was a deck and a fountain and a small pond. "The water isn't flowing right," Chantal's father said. "Something must be blocked." He put on rubber boots and climbed into the pond. He laid his tools on the edge of the water. He spent the rest of the afternoon trying to fix the fountain, standing in the water, standing in the mud.

. . .

After Charlie died, I stopped praying. Prayer for me had been like a reflex, like breathing or blinking—*Please keep us safe, please keep us safe, please keep us safe*—but it felt wrong now, every time. I had prayed for Charlie. So had hundreds of people. But he died.

When I tell it like that, it sounds like I stopped praying out of spite or anger, a bratty child who didn't get her way saying, *You didn't answer my prayers, God, so now I'll stop praying. Take that!* But that's not what happened.

This is what happened:

Before Charlie died, God was still my secret comfort. I criticized the father-figure God by day, but at night, when I was alone, I prayed to him, this man who thought I was special, who chose me, protected me, kept me safe, well, loved. My God was still a God who could hear me, a God with the power to make some sick and others well, to intervene in soccer matches, to influence the outcome of wars.

Intellectually, I had never been able to square my secret God with what I'd learned at school or with what I read in newspapers—but the dissonance hadn't stopped me from praying. I still wanted to be held by that God rather than not being held by anything at all. I still wanted God's blessing.

But belief in blessing has an underside. If you believe in a God who blesses, you also believe in a God who curses, condemns. *Yes, we've been blessed*, people say, and now what I hear is: *God chose me.* For this Mercedes. For this big house on the hill. For this remission. And you? He chose poverty for you. And war. And a bomb on your child's kindergarten playground. And a tsunami. And cancer. *God must have needed another angel. God works in mysterious ways.*

But then Charlie died, and the devil's third temptation in the desert suddenly made sense to me. On the pinnacle of a temple he says to Jesus, *If you are the Son of God, throw yourself down from here.* The devil talks about the promise of angels, of protection, of not dashing his foot against a stone, but Jesus says, *Do not put the Lord your God to the test.*

I think Jesus knew if he jumped, he would fall. His God wouldn't catch him. There was just too much suffering in the world—too many people drowning in floods and buried by earthquakes, too many people starving, too many people sick and dying for Jesus to believe in a God who'd catch someone who jumped off a building to prove a point to a bully.

I had believed in a God who loved me, and because he loved me, and because I was good, he would protect me. My faith was a kind of magic trick. My prayers were not much different from incantations. I might as well have been saying *abracadabra*. I might as well have been standing on the top of a temple, arms spread wide, leaping into the air.

. . .

Refusing to pray made working at a church difficult. When I was not in the basement with the children during Sunday school, I sat at the front of the church, next to the choir, facing the congregation. Everyone could see me, so I mouthed the words like a kid in choir who has forgotten the words and sings *watermelon cantaloupe watermelon cantaloupe* because a friend once told her that doing that would make it look like she was singing the right words. I knew it was juvenile to believe mouthing words instead of speaking them gave me some sort of integrity, so I soon stopped even mouthing the words. I bent my head. I closed my eyes.

People in the congregation regularly asked me to pray for them, and I didn't think their requests should be met with an explanation of why I thought intercessory prayer was fucked up, so instead I said, *I will keep you in my thoughts. I will hold you in the light.*

The only other prayer I had left was gratitude. *Thank you thank you thank you*, I said all day long, every day. I didn't know who or what I was thanking, but, for some reason, it didn't seem to matter.

I was back in school again, in the doctoral program in theology at Harvard, and I took every class Gordon Kaufman taught and signed up for independent studies with him, reading and research courses on philosophical and theological understandings of imagination, on creativity, on theology and art.

I spent many afternoons in Kaufman's office, a small room in the basement of Andover Hall with a single window looking out onto a pile of dirt and squirrels and the roots of an elm tree. He sat in a rocking chair, and I told him about my experience at the church, how frustrating it was, how out of place I felt. It was his version of God I had brought with me to church—serendipitous creativity—and I wanted his help. I wanted him to soothe my grief, to relieve my disappointment. I wanted him to help me find a way to pray again, to feel at home in institutional Christianity. "How am I going to be a priest?" I asked.

"People are in cages of their own making," he said. "I can stand on the outside of the cage and show them the gate is unlocked, that they are free to go, that they have always been free to go, but they need to decide to leave the cage."

At the time I thought he was talking about the people in the congregation where I worked, but I see now he was talking about me.

. . .

Sometimes you break up with the person you love because you discover he isn't who you thought he was. Maybe he has wives in other cities. Maybe he runs a Ponzi scheme. Maybe you walk in on him fucking someone else. Or maybe he's just different when he's around other people. Maybe when he's with his friends or when he thinks you're not around to hear him, he makes racist jokes or catcalls women or threatens to kill someone who accidentally bumps into him at a bar. Sometimes the reasons for breaking up aren't so dramatic. Maybe it's just how he chews his cereal or the way he breathes through his mouth when he's reading the newspaper or his habit of turning on the television first thing in the morning when he isn't even in the room to hear the bad news and you are in the room and you're trying to write in your journal.

Sometimes you stay because you think you can fix him, because you think he'll change, because you remember the good times, the plans you made, everything you thought was possible. You try to correct his sexist language, deconstruct his racist jokes, show him how his homophobia is problematic, point out places in the world that need his attention, places he could make a difference. You convince yourself that he doesn't seem to mind, that he likes changing, that he'll do anything to stay with you because he loves you and wants to make this work, and pretty soon he's doing all the right things, saying all the sweet words you've been longing to hear, and changing him feels good, even empowering, but then, all of a sudden, it's terrifying because when you look at him, all you see is what you projected onto him, and you realize that he's miserable, that you're turning him into someone he's not, someone he doesn't want to be, and that everything you thought you loved about him is really everything you want to love about yourself.

So you decide to move out. You pack up all your stuff when he's not home, and you're gone by the time he gets back. You call him from your sister's house and mumble something about people changing, about wanting different things, about needing to be apart in order to be together someday, about reclaiming yourselves as whole people so you don't die on the inside or end up hating each other or drowning in resentment. Deep down you want him to stop you from leaving, you want him to promise things will be different, you want him to beg you to come back home, but he doesn't. He doesn't say a word.

One night I finally pushed my discernment committee far enough that they suggested maybe I didn't really want to be a priest, that if I was going to be like that, if I was going to keep saying that God was in our imaginations and that Christianity could have been much better than it was, then maybe this wasn't the best job for me, maybe I was called to other work in the world. At the end of the meeting, I blew out the candle we'd lit at the beginning of the meeting and walked to my car, its bumper backed up against a wall, and drove away, Coldplay's "Shiver" on repeat. I felt like Chris Martin was singing to me, singing about changing, about not being seen, about waiting for what would never arrive. Soon I was crying so hard I had trouble seeing the road. I needed to talk to someone, so I called my friend Eric and told him between sobs what happened. "I don't think you should be driving like this," he said. "Why don't you pull over?" I pulled over and cried with Eric on the other end of the phone line. I told him I was crying because of what had happened during the meeting, but I was also crying because I knew it was over between me and God, and I knew I would be the one to end it.

. . .

I broke up with God that night. I broke up with the priesthood. I broke up with the river and the sky opening and the dove calling me beloved. I broke up with chosenness and salvation and belonging. And I imagined God held me while I cried.

I can't do this anymore, I said. *I'm not happy.*

I know, I heard him say. *I know.*

I dropped out of the ordination process and then out of Christianity altogether, but I didn't tell anyone it was over between God and me, not my friends, not my parents, not my professors at school, not myself. I told people I stopped trying to be a priest because the church was sexist and inflexible, but the truth was I stopped trying to be a priest because I fell out of love, maybe with God, maybe with myself. "How's your relationship with God?" people asked. "Great," I said. "We're doing great."

I went back to the places I used to go with God, trying to get that feeling back, trying to remember what being in love felt like, but it was like visiting "It's a Small World" at Disneyland when you're an adult: the magic's gone, and all you can see is racism and dirty water and poorly made dolls spinning around and around, going nowhere. I tried to remember what I felt when I was with him when things were good between us—all those feelings of belonging, of being chosen—but I couldn't feel it anymore. I cried a lot, I got migraines, and I felt like such a cliché. In my attempt to change God I had changed myself. I turned myself into exactly the person I thought he wanted me to be, a theologian, a preacher, a teacher, and I ended up abandoned and alone, lost, confused about who I was, about what I was supposed to do.

People kept asking me to lead prayers, to say grace before family meals, to officiate at their weddings, to preach at their churches, and I did, but I didn't bring God with me to these events. All I could talk about was love, the mystery of it.

. . .

I started a Women-Church community at the divinity school so I could have one place to go where the liturgy wouldn't make me throw up, where I wouldn't feel more pissed off and anxious after the service than I did when I first arrived. I e-mailed women I knew, put up signs around Harvard's campus and in coffee shops, wrote a new liturgy. We met monthly in Andover Chapel, arranged the chairs in a circle, read poems, tried experimental rituals, made art together. *Welcome. This is woman space. Welcome. This is sacred space. Welcome. This is find-god-in-yourself-and-love-her-fiercely space. This is every-true-thing-is-okay space. This is embodied space. Safe space. Dance space. Free space. Nonviolent space. Political space. Resistant space. Cry space. Laugh space. Hope space. Welcome. This is your space. Dream it into being.*

I was also part of a small group of women that had been meeting regularly for several years, and soon after I dropped out of the ordination process at the church, the three other women in that group—Ann, Laura, and Tovis—ordained me. *You don't need a church to be a minister,* they said. *You are called to let your light shine in the world, to be your best, biggest self, and to remember that you are always beloved.* I took vows, promising to work for peace and justice, to care for the world and for myself. They anointed me, blessed me. They claimed me as a minister when I could not claim myself.

A few months later, Tovis asked me and Laura—an ordained United Church of Christ minister—to officiate at her wedding in New Hampshire. The day before the ceremony, I was napping in my room in a cabin on the shore of a lake when Eric came into the room yelling, "Get up! Get up! Does your cell phone work here? Call 911!" He had been on a run around the lake and was running downhill while two people—a man and a woman—were riding their bikes uphill. The woman was in front of the man and reached Eric first. Eric cheered for her—"Way to go!" he said—and then he watched the man, several feet behind her, pedal once, stop pedaling, and fall over onto the ground, into the middle of the street. The woman heard him fall, and she and Eric ran to him. "Please," she said. "Find a phone and call 911." Eric got on her bike and rode back to the cabin where we were staying.

I put on shoes and called 911 while we ran back to where the man had fallen. By the time we arrived, an ambulance was already there. A paramedic had driven past where the man had fallen, and he was still trying to resuscitate him. The woman was sitting on the side of the road, no one else around her. "Maybe she'd like a minister," I said to Eric and walked over to her. I put my hand gently on her back. "Would you like a minister?" I asked.

"Yes," she said. "Oh, yes. Please."

"I'll send someone to go get one," I said.

I found Eric. "She wants a minister," I said. "Go get Laura."

"But you're a minister," he said. "That's why you're at this wedding."

"I think she wants a real one," I said.

Eric ran to get Laura, and I sat next to the woman and held her hand. "I just want him to breathe," she said. "He wasn't breathing."

"Let's breathe together," I said. So we breathed. In and out, in and out, my hand on her back, just behind her heart.

"Heavenly Father, be with him," she said.

Laura arrived just as the woman and I were climbing into the front seat of a truck that would take us to the hospital, following the ambulance. "You didn't need me," Laura said. "You're a minister, remember? I ordained you."

Then Laura got into the truck with us, and the three of us breathed together. "I just want him to breathe," the woman said. "Please, Heavenly Father. I just want him to breathe."

At the hospital, they ushered the three of us into a small room on the side of the regular emergency waiting room. There was a light blue couch and a Bible on a coffee table in the corner of the room. "Will you read something?" she asked. I chose a Psalm randomly. *Let everything that breathes praise the Lord*, I read.

The woman started crying. "He's a good man," she said. "But he's not a believer. He hasn't accepted Jesus Christ. I'm afraid he won't go to heaven." She turned to me. "I'm so afraid," she said. "Will God let him in?"

"Yes," I said. "I'm sure of it."

A man came into the room, wearing a white coat. "Are you his wife?" the doctor asked the woman.

"Yes," she said.

"I'm sorry," he said.

. . .

I needed to get away. I drove four hours from Boston to Tenants Harbor, Maine, to spend three days at Greenfire, a retreat center founded by women who were priests and felt lonely and isolated in the profession. They wanted to find other ways to minister to people, other ways to be in community. Some of them were among the first women ever ordained in the Episcopal Church, a group known as the Philadelphia Eleven, heroes of mine.

I arrived in the early evening, in the rain, and before I even got out of my car, I knew I was in the right place—a two-hundred-year-old farmhouse in the middle of a meadow, surrounded by woods, so near the ocean I could smell the salt in the air. I walked to the front door, and a woman welcomed me. She was making peach cobbler for dinner, and she wiped her hands on her apron, led me through the kitchen where a group of women was cooking green beans and corn on the cob, and brought me to my room. I had arrived in time for the evening meditation, she said, and I could come downstairs in a few minutes if I felt like joining the circle, or I could just come down when I was ready for dinner.

My room was pink and tiny, six feet by six feet, with a slanted ceiling so low that I couldn't stand up in most parts of it. There was no room for my suitcase, so I unpacked what I needed—books, my journal, my favorite pen, a water bottle, a lavender eye pillow—and slid my suitcase under the bed.

I went downstairs, wrapped myself in an afghan, and joined the meditation circle. After thirty minutes of silence, the woman leading the meditation asked, "What is the purpose of human beings on the earth?"

There is no purpose, I thought but stayed quiet while other women offered different answers to her question.

I was at Greenfire for a "WorkVision." Every day for three days I would sit with three other women—

Connie, Chambliss, and Alison—who would, the brochure said, *listen me into being.*

As soon as my first session started I cried. I told them about the little girl at the church who died. I told them about Charlie. I told them about leaving the ordination process. I told them about feeling like I'd lost God. They listened for a long time, without interrupting, and then Connie said, "You're grieving." I knew I was sad, but I thought I felt so miserable because I had done something wrong, made a mistake, ruined everything. "Your grief is wrapped in shame," she said. "But grief can lead to freedom. It can heal you."

After the first session, they handed me some wet clay and told me to sculpt myself as a little girl and to bring my sculpture to our session the following day. I sat on the lawn and created myself. Braids. A protective shell, which then became a cape. Soccer cleats.

During the second session, they asked me what I was trying to avoid. *A void*, I thought. I was avoiding the enormous emptiness at my center, a deep dark pit full of sticky thick tar. I was avoiding sitting still because I knew if I let myself rest I would never get up again. I was avoiding grief because if I started crying I would cry forever. I was avoiding my fear that I was ordinary, that I wasn't chosen. I was avoiding being a writer because I thought I had nothing worth saying, because I thought writing wouldn't do anyone any good, because it didn't involve enough struggle.

"Don't be afraid of what comes easily to you," Alison said.

At the end of the second session, they sent me to a lighthouse near the retreat center. "Just sit there," they said. "Your only job is to just be. You're not allowed to do anything else—not even write in your journal."

During the final session, they performed a ritual they had designed just for me. They brushed my hair. They gave me a small shell so I could listen to the sound of the sea, the earth's breath. They anointed my feet, my heart, my hands. *The hands of a writer*, they said.

On the drive back to Boston, I drove over a bridge and when I reached the other side I pulled onto the shoulder of the road and parked. I walked to the edge of the ocean and threw my little girl self into the water.

Rainer Maria Rilke's God

I love you, gentlest of Ways,
who ripened us as we wrestled with you.

You, the great homesickness we could never shake off,
you, the forest that always surrounded us,

you, the song we sang in every silence,
you dark net threading through us,

on the day you made us you created yourself,
and we grew sturdy in your sunlight. . .

Let your hand rest on the rim of heaven now
and mutely bear the darkness we bring over you.

After I finally admitted that I broke up with God, Eric took me to the desert to hike in the deep canyons of Utah. Terry Tempest Williams writes that when you first encounter Utah's deserts you expect them to bleed. All that red—soil, rock, bloom. In the desert I heard the earth say, *Everything you can do to me I have already done to myself.* Cracked. Split open. Drowned.

I know why Jesus went to the desert. The desert doesn't pretend. It doesn't ask you to be something you're not because it doesn't care who you are. It would let you die. You can feel small. You can disappear. What are you next to carved canyons, lifted reefs, oceans that arrive and recede and return only to vanish again?

Before I went to the desert, I imagined Jesus in an expanse of sandy emptiness, but for those forty days he was surrounded by wildness. For him, acacia tree, jackal, desert fox, white oryx, black basalt. For me, red-tailed hawks, sandstone, sego lily, desert whiptail, storm cloud, flash flood.

Bread. Flight. Power. It's easy to refuse what you already know you don't need. It's harder to refuse what you believe you need. Each of us "carries a tender spot: something our lives forgot to give us," writes the poet Naomi Shihab Nye. Real temptation speaks to this tenderness, promises to fill that hollow.

The desert is haunted by the ocean. I stood in Little Wild Horse Canyon and traced the outline a shell left on the wall. *This is what my insides must look like,* I thought. God carved the shape of me and then disappeared. Wavy waterless waterway. Climb down the wash. Enter the narrows.

The desert sky was filled with vultures circling. They eat what we leave behind. I imagined they found the remnants of my faith and carried it high. When I die, I would like to be reduced to bone by them. The closest we can get to resurrection is this: borrowed flight on black wings.

6

SEEING OTHER PEOPLE

Twice I've had dreams in which I meet another person and feel connected, complete. I had the first when I was in high school. I'm on a ship, a ferry, and I meet a man in a small blue hallway. We know we're meant to be together. We hold each other, and I feel at home, deep peace, belonging.

I had the second dream when I was living in Cambridge. I'm competing in a theological karaoke contest—really—and the challenge is to sing a song that captures the essence of different theologians' work. I'm assigned Jürgen Moltmann. I sing, the audience cheers, and when I return to the table, Moltmann sits right next to me. *No one has ever understood me like you understand me,* he says. He leans his leg into mine under the table, and I have the same feeling I had on the boat.

I told Martina, my therapist, about the karaoke dream. "I want to fall in love with someone who makes me feel like Moltmann did," I said. "I want to feel that way all the time."

"That dream isn't about finding someone to love you," Martina said.

"What?" I said. "Of course it is."

"You are every person in your dream," she said. "You are the audience. You are yourself. And you are Moltmann."

"I don't want to be every person in the dream," I said.

"That dream is telling you that you don't need someone else to give you that feeling," Martina said. "You can do it for yourself. It's already yours."

But I didn't want to do it for myself. I wanted someone else to do it for me. Someone else to rescue me. From my shame. From my fear. From myself.

That someone used to be God.

. . .

Before the art building at Greenhill School was the art building it was the elementary school. Before the elementary school, it was a turkey farm. Before a turkey farm, Blackland prairie. Buffalo grass, pigeon berry, meadow sedge, little bluestem, Indian grass, blue grama, green sprangletop. Now, no prairie, no turkeys—only peacocks, as if the turkeys had been transformed into gods, surprising us with their iridescent blue extravagance, their hundred eyes, their rooftop keening.

When I was a student there, the art building had some farm life left. Rats and skunks and raccoons lived beneath it, an elaborate underspace of tunnels and nests. During class, the art teacher arranged fruits and vegetables on a table at the front for students to paint. At night, the animals came up into the emptiness to carry off pieces of each still life. An apple, an onion, a cluster of grapes. In the morning, the half-painted, still-wet fruits and vegetables on the canvases were the only evidence that the food had ever existed.

After I broke up with God, I still had all the language of my faith—*salvation, resurrection, crucifixion, savior, sin, grace, Christian, priest*—but I couldn't make it mean anything anymore. I felt like I did when I was a child and said certain words over and over again until they dissolved into sound and meaninglessness. *Chocolate chocolatechocolatechocolate. Enoughenoughenoughenough enough. Christianchristianchristianchristian. Saviorsavior saviorsaviorsavior.* If humans are the animals who believe the stories we tell about ourselves, what happens when we stop believing our stories?

My grandfather had Alzheimer's. We watched him unravel, lose nouns, names. At the end, he couldn't feed or bathe or dress himself. He didn't recognize his son and daughter. But once in a while, a favorite phrase was found: "Hot damn," he said, pushing his walker ahead of him, his words like liturgy, like light.

My grandfather rarely said *I love you*. "I love you, Grandpa," we'd say when we were children. "Okay," he'd say. "Alright."

Alzheimer's stole everything from my grandfather and offered him gentleness in return. He let us touch him, comb his soft white hair, hold his hand, rub his back. My father knelt beside his father, forehead to forehead, whispering.

Years ago, my grandfather built an electric train set for my brother. Laid tracks on a wood table that fit over my brother's second twin bed. Planted a forest of trees. Station. Curves. Switches. Motion. Light.

They say the brain is like a railroad. A protein called tau keeps the tracks straight. In a brain with Alzheimer's, tau collapses in twisted strands. Cells die. The cortex shrivels and shrinks while ventricles expand, creating crevasses no train can pass over. Tau, the nineteenth letter of the Greek alphabet, the shape of the cross, symbol of resurrection, symbol of death.

It often seemed as if there was something my grandfather wanted to say but couldn't, something he needed to tell us but didn't know how. We thought he'd lost language, but now I wonder if he knew the right word but the word didn't seem up to the task anymore. It meant too much, or it didn't mean enough. Good-bye *chair*, I imagine he thought, pointing at his blue easy chair. Good-bye *Vera*, I imagine he thought, lying in the hospital bed they wheeled next to his marriage bed. Good-bye *home* and *dog* and *death*. He rode his mind around the bend, past the twisted heaps, through the forest of dead and blooming branches, past the station-master with his striped hat and raised arm, and over the deep.

What makes us who we are? The words we say? The things we do? My grandfather completed the *New York Times* crossword puzzle in ink every day. He ate ice cream with a knife and fork to make his grandchildren laugh. He built birdhouses and chairs and dollhouses in his workshop. Do our brains make us who we are? One hundred billion brain cells and their branches connecting at one hundred trillion points? Routine? Pattern? Electricity? Plaques and tangles?

Scientists recently studied the brains of Buddhist monks and named one "the happiest man in the world." The label makes him laugh. Before he was a monk, he was a French scientist, but then he watched a documentary film on Tibetan spiritual teachers, and their meditating faces changed his life. He knew that even if he became the greatest scientist in the history of the world his face would never look like theirs. He left the Pasteur Institute for the Himalayas.

Happiness lives in the prefrontal cortex of our brains, on the left, and despair lives on the right. Scientists attached electrodes to the monk's skull so they could see inside it. They wanted to know what ten thousand hours sitting on a mat might do. I imagine they stood close to the monitor and watched gamma waves like they had never seen before. The monk's left prefrontal cortex was swollen, enlarged, but his right was shriveled, small, as if the capacity for sadness could simply disappear.

Look, I imagine they said. *Joy.*

Plasticity: Thoughts can change the brain. The brain can change the body. When I think of chocolate cake, my mouth waters. When I think of heat, I sweat. When I think of Jesus, I hold my hands in front of my face and look for the marks nails make. When I think of God. . .

If what we think might save us, then I will think of flight, of seed, of song. I will think of birds—this bird: She flew into the closed window of our house and fell straight down into snow. We looked through the glass. "I think she's dead," I said. We waited and watched. She didn't move. I walked into the air and cold. I wanted to bury her, to dig a grave in the icy ground and cover her with leaves and dirt and snow. I leaned over the small still bird. And then she flew away, so close I felt her wings on my face.

. . .

I fell in love. With a real human being. Eric and I met during my second year of divinity school, his first. Katie and I were working at the orientation table, and I handed him his registration packet and made friendly small talk. He had just moved to Cambridge from Santa Barbara, where he'd been a middle-school teacher. We compared notes about Southern California and teaching and talked about which classes we were going to take that semester. "Cute," Katie and I both said when he left to go look through the course catalog. "I wish I wasn't wearing overalls," I added. I'd come from the studio, my clothes and shoes splattered with paint.

Eric and I were friends first, spending almost every weekend studying together in the art library. We passed notes back and forth like we were in middle school, laughing so hard we had to go outside, and once, our eyes met, and I thought, *This is the person I'm going to marry*, but quickly pushed that thought out of my mind. I wasn't ready.

He wasn't ready either. He'd left behind a train wreck of a relationship in California and needed time to heal, which translated into needing time to date a lot of other women. And it was that familiar scent of unavailability that drew me to him.

"I think I like you more than a friend," I said one afternoon in his apartment while we were both reading Paul Tillich, and before he could respond I rushed out of his apartment. I'd promised my friend I would go to the chapel to hear her sing holiday songs with the divinity school choir.

I walked home in the rain after the concert. *What have I done?* I thought, but then there was a knock on my door, and it was Eric, glasses fogged up from the rain, and he took my face in his hands and kissed me.

But we still weren't ready for each other. He wasn't done with other women, and I wasn't done feeling unlovable, so we gave each other exactly what we needed. Pain and heartache and drama and dishonesty. And when we'd finally both had enough, it was the end of the school year, and I went to Idaho to spend the summer with my brother.

There's a story I heard about a woman who's starving. A man comes to her door with a pizza. "You can have this pizza if you let me control your life," he says.

"Come in, come in," the woman says.

But now imagine the woman has a kitchen filled with food, a magical kitchen in which she can create whatever she desires. A man comes to the door with a pizza. "You can have this pizza if you let me control your life," he says.

"No thank you," she says. "There is room for you at this feast, but my life belongs to me."

. . .

I came back to Cambridge believing I was free of Eric—even though I'd spent most of the summer thinking about him—and then we bumped into each other on the street and he invited me to dinner. I walked to our favorite restaurant, telling myself it was still over, that I could do better, that I could be with someone who wanted to be with me. I promised myself the only way I would even entertain the possibility of getting back together with him was if he said, *I want you and only you.*

We sat down to dinner. "I want you and only you," he said.

Our do-over was rough going at first. I was often accusatory, brimming with venom, ready for him to prove I wasn't lovable. He'd listen, quietly, as I yelled about what he wasn't doing, or what he was doing, or what he should be doing if he really loved me. When I finished, exhausted, he'd say, "I think this has nothing to do with me." He'd kiss me gently on the forehead. "I'll be at my house having a beer when you're ready," he'd say, closing the door softly behind him.

Forced to soothe myself, I learned I was the only one who could fill the emptiness inside me. If I didn't love myself, I wouldn't be able to love anyone else. I wouldn't be able to receive love, either. *You are your beloved. With yourself be well pleased.*

I was still writing morning pages every morning, and during the first year Eric and I were together—what we now call "year zero"—my journal was all about him. What I needed to do to convince him to be in an exclusive relationship with me. What I needed to do to make him love me. What I needed to wear or think or say to make him want to be with me. But when we got back together after my summer in Idaho, my morning pages weren't about him anymore. They were about me. About the work I wanted to do in the world. About how I could live a life that mattered.

The first version of Eric I met was a decoy. He looked and acted and sounded exactly like other men I'd been willing to sacrifice myself for, and it was that likeness that drew me to him, but it was not the real Eric but a version of himself he'd constructed in response to heartache and betrayal. It was almost as if I were a drug addict who'd fallen for my dealer, only to discover he wasn't a dealer at all but a counselor who could help cure me of my habit.

And it also wasn't like that at all. We were both counselors and we were both addicts and we were both healers.

All my life I'd been willing to open the door to anyone who promised to feed me the story I was used to, but now I was writing a new story, and in this story, I was the protagonist of my own life.

I had never been loved so well.

We moved into a third-floor apartment in a tri-decker near Porter Square whose walls we painted in bright colors—turmeric, oxblood, cobalt. We turned the second bedroom into a shared office crammed full with two big desks, several overflowing bookcases, file cabinets, and a reading chair. Our landlord converted her garage into a studio for me so that I would have a place to paint.

Eric had been keeping a vegetarian home for close to a decade when I met him, so when we moved in together, I agreed to be vegetarian at home, too. We still ate meat in restaurants or if it was served to us by other people, but in our apartment we cooked no meat. I consented to this arrangement, but I found it a bit strange, even embarrassing. I'm from Texas. Eating meat at every meal is a "national" pastime. My family found our vegetarian household particularly odd. *Why in the world wouldn't you eat meat at home?*

It's a Sentilles tradition to prepare too much food, and whenever we visited my family, Eric would eat the leftover meat the following day even though the rest us had moved on to whatever new meat dish was next. My mother or father would pull me aside. "He doesn't have to eat those leftovers," they'd say. "There's plenty of fresh food for everyone."

"But this is an animal," Eric would say when I told him what they said. "A life. Flesh. I'm not going to waste it. I'm not going to just throw it in the trash."

We laughed at him. We rolled our eyes. We quoted bumper stickers: *If we're not supposed to eat animals, why are they made out of meat?* We quoted the *Simpsons* episode when Lisa becomes a vegetarian:

"Lisa, honey, are you saying you're never going to eat any animal again?" Homer asks. "What about bacon?"

"No," Lisa says.

"Ham?"

"No."

"Pork chops?"

"No. Dad, those all come from the same animal."

"Yeah right, Lisa. A wonderful, magical animal."

When I was teaching elementary school in Compton, one of my students was tested for the district's gifted and talented program, and the examiners asked, "Where do hamburgers come from?"

"From the grocery store," he answered, which was not the right answer—*cows* was the right answer—but it was the answer I also would have given. The grocery story was where I believed all food came from. Carrots and broccoli and asparagus grew in piles in the produce aisle. Raspberries and strawberries ripened in plastic packaging stacked in pyramids near the front of the store where they were available all year long. Turkeys lived in the glass cases of the deli waiting to be sliced thinly for my sandwiches. Milk and cheese came from the refrigerated dairy section. I was completely disconnected from my food—where it grew, when it grew, how it grew, the amount of labor it took to produce it, the chemicals used, how farmworkers were treated, how animals were treated. I never gave any of that a single thought. *I had an eating disorder, but now look at me!* I ate what I wanted to eat when I wanted to eat it.

But then Eric and I joined a community-supported agriculture program through Bay End Farm in Buzzard's Bay, Massachusetts, and every week, two of the farmers, Erin and Kofi, delivered a bag of organic vegetables, freshly baked bread, recipes, and a bouquet of just-picked flowers to our front porch. Eggplants. Bok choy. Radishes. Yellow carrots. Jerusalem artichokes. Heads of romaine. Receiving that bag was like a revelation, like connecting the dots. *Holy shit! Food grows on farms! Carrots are roots!* It was like learning to eat all over again.

The farmers always rang our doorbell when they delivered our weekly share of produce, and I would sprint down three flights of stairs to try to catch them before they climbed into their truck and drove away. I almost never made it, but I'd stand on my porch waving both arms anyway, shouting, "Thank you! Thank you! Thank you!"

I had been living in denial, cut off from what fed me. *They know not what they do.* Pretending things are not as we know them to be is exhausting. Deadening one thought requires deadening most thought. "How does the Tylenol know where to go?" a friend's daughter asked. Pork is pig. Beef is cow. Carrots are roots. *Take. Eat. This is my body.*

Kofi and Erin must have sometimes spent the night in Cambridge on food drop days before returning to the farm in Buzzard's Bay because once I saw Erin in my yoga class the morning after she left the bag of produce on our front porch. I watched her practice. Downward dog. Upward dog. Child's pose. Wheel. *She grows my food*, I thought, tears running down my face. *She grows my food!*

When Erin noticed that I was staring at her and crying, I waved and smiled, and after class I introduced myself. "You grow my food!" I said, as if that explained my strange behavior.

. . .

During my final semester of coursework at Harvard, the photographs taken by American guards at Abu Ghraib prison in Iraq were published, and I saw the picture of the man hooded, standing on a cardboard box, arms stretched out, wires attached to his hands. I couldn't go on pretending I hadn't seen it.

I decided to write about those photographs, about torture. I had been preparing to write a dissertation on imagination, but that photograph confronted me with my complicity in the pictured violence in a way other images of violence had not, even other photographs that also showed violence sanctioned by U.S. policies. Rendering the photograph even more arresting to me was the fact that the man on the box stood in a crucifixion-like position. Christianity had something to do with this violence. I had something to do with this violence.

An American's God

The second day they transferred Ameen Sa'eed Al-Sheikh to the hard site. A soldier put a sandbag over his head. He didn't see anything after that. They took him inside the building and started to scream at him. They stripped him naked. "Do you pray to Allah?" they asked him. "Yes," he said. "Fuck you," they said. "And fuck him."

The guards beat his broken leg. They threatened to rape him and his wife. They threatened to kill him, put a gun to his head, deprived him of blankets and clothing, drew pictures of women on his back, made him stand naked and hold his buttocks, urinated on him, hung him from his bed using handcuffs until he lost consciousness, hung him from the cell door, took photographs of him, forced him to eat pork and to drink liquor.

Someone else asked him, "Do you believe in anything?"

"I believe in Allah," he said.

"But I believe in torture and I will torture you."

Then they handcuffed him and hung him from his bed. They ordered him to curse Islam and because they hit his broken leg, he cursed his religion. They ordered him to thank Jesus he was alive. And he did what they ordered him to do, which was against his belief.

After two years of coursework, it was time for me to take general exams—three days of written examinations and one oral exam during which I would be tested on the hundreds of books listed on the three bibliographies I had constructed with the help of my adviser and dissertation committee. I had four months to prepare. One of my exams would be on theological method, another on knowledge of God with a sub-specialty in feminist theologies, and the final one would be on philosophical and theological understandings of imagination with a focus on how viewers respond to images of violence. To be able to write about the photographs from Abu Ghraib, I had to immerse myself in fields I hadn't studied before—photography theory, visual culture, response theory, ethics and aesthetics, and violence—and I used my third exam as an opportunity to learn that new material.

During those months of preparation, you could find me in one of two places—my carrel in the basement of Andover-Harvard Theological Library or the yoga studio down the street from our apartment. Studying for the first two exams—reading all the major Christian theological texts in chronological order—was like reading old love letters between me and God, like sorting through photographs and e-mails and voice messages, trying to figure out where our relationship had gone wrong. *But we were so happy.*

Looking at photographs of my relatives who have died—my grandfather sitting in a cart pulled by his pet donkey, my grandmother on her wedding day, my great-grandparents kneeling in the grass, holding me so I can smell a rose—I feel uneasy. I know something they will never know: how the end will come.

Someone told me Judy Garland committed suicide, and when I watched *The Wizard of Oz* as a child, I couldn't stop staring at her. *Don't do it, don't do it, don't do it,* I thought, as if my secret message could reach her, could save her.

Mother, my grandfather cried as the Alzheimer's worsened. *Take me home.*

There's no place like home.

I practiced yoga early in the morning before the sun was up. I walked to the studio in the dark to sweat through the same series of movements. Once, while we were in frog position—difficult and painful for me to hold—my yoga teacher told us about her experience giving birth to her first child. In terrible pain, she turned to her mother in the delivery room and said, *I want to go home.*

You have to stay, her mother said. *You have to finish this.*

My teacher said she had never wanted to get out of something so badly, and she had never had to stay for something that was so painful. There was no alternative. She had to finish what she started. And at the end, new life. "Part of life," she said, "is discerning when you need to stay and when it's time to go. Sometimes it's difficult to tell the difference."

With my legs bent behind me, my hips screaming, my forehead on the floor, I wondered if I should have stayed in the ordination process. Had I given up too easily? Could I have made my relationship with God work? Could I have saved it? Should I try to find another church? Should I switch denominations? Had I made the right decision to leave? Had I ruined my life? Was God angry with me? Did I care?

. . .

For three days in Widener Library, I took my general exams, and every night Eric made his special enchiladas, my favorite meal. A week after my last exam I sat in a room with my dissertation committee and they asked me questions about the essays I'd written and then said, "Congratulations, Sarah. You passed." I walked out of the examination room to find Eric sitting in a lawn chair at the end of the hallway holding a sign that said "Boyfriend of Ms. SmartyPants," rolls of Smarties glued all over his clothing.

Eric and I got engaged, we got married in a ceremony next to a river, and we decided to move to Idaho, where Eric would write his dissertation and a book about adolescent development, and I would write a book about sexism and women's experiences working in churches. We met our moving truck in Idaho and nearly froze while two men unloaded almost all of our belongings into a storage space during a snowstorm. We had marked some boxes "storage front" and others "storage back." My "storage front" boxes were filled with my favorite novels. Eric suggested it might be a better idea to put things we might actually need in the front of our storage space. "Haven't you read them all already?" he asked.

"So?" I said. I wanted my novels near me, in case I needed to read them again, in case I needed to look something up, which seemed like a perfectly reasonable idea until we had to move out of a furnished place and into our own apartment and tried to find our knives and pots and pans.

When we first arrived in Idaho, friends from Cambridge would ask, "How's Utah?"

"Idaho," I'd say, gently, having rediscovered my patience by watching the moon rise and adhering to the twenty-five mile-per-hour speed limit in town. Several people, including my adviser, thought I was living in Iowa. I corrected one friend, telling her I was living in Idaho, not Iowa, and she said, "Well, the only thing I know for sure about Idaho is that Robert Redford lives there."

"He lives in Utah," I said.

"Potatoes?" she asked.

In Idaho I read Michael Pollan's *The Omnivore's Dilemma* and learned that the Food and Drug Administration (FDA), the organization charged with protecting and promoting our health, with keeping our food safe, is not protecting or promoting our health at all. Many of the government's policies around food production are designed not for wellness but for profit—for the corporations that process food, not for the people who grow it. The FDA has okayed, for example, adding dimethylpolysiloxane to the cooking oil in which some chicken nuggets are fried—a suspected carcinogen and an established mutagen, tumorigen, and reproductive effector. It's also, Pollan writes, flammable. Even more alarming, however, is the fact that tertiary butylhydroquinone—or TBHQ, an antioxidant derived from petroleum—is sprayed directly onto the nugget or onto the inside of the box it comes in to "help preserve freshness." TBHQ is a form of butane—read: lighter fluid—and the FDA allows processors to use it in our food. "It can comprise no more than 0.02 percent of the oil in a nugget," Pollan writes. "Which is probably just as well, considering that ingesting a single gram of TBHQ can cause 'nausea, vomiting, ringing in the ears, delirium, a sense of suffocation, and collapse.' Ingesting five grams of TBHQ can kill."

"We're being poisoned!" I shouted to Eric who was brushing his teeth. I usually read Pollan's book in bed, screaming or crying, often forcing Eric to listen to long passages I read out loud. "Did you know there are no pigtails in industrial hog production?" I shouted and then explained what I'd learned—how farmers wean piglets from their mothers too early, leaving them with a lifelong craving to suck and chew. Confined—no dirt, no sun, no straw, just metal and concrete and shit below—they chew the tail of the pig in front of them, and that pig has no desire to stop the chewing. He lets the pig suckle until his tail gets infected. How else can the pig call the butchers to him? How else end his own life? How else get *clubbed to death on the spot*? This pig with an infected tail is now a problem for the farmer, lost income. The farmer's solution? Removing all pigs' tails with pliers. No anesthetic. He knows not to cut too much. He leaves a stump more sensitive than the spiraled tail. Then a bite from the pig behind will be so painful even a depressed pig will resist it.

I played my part in this slaughter. How many turkeys had I eaten in my lifetime? How many pigs? How many cows? How many chickens? How much pain had my food choices caused? I thought about the veal farms in Idaho, picket fences and rows of miniature white houses, a parody of suburbia I drove right by.

Friends invited us to their house for Thanksgiving. I ate a big helping of free-range turkey. "Did you know—" I started.

"No, Sarah," Eric said. "Not now."

It was my last meal of meat.

An Ecologist's God

When we believe something, we are saying we think that reality is like *this* more than it is like *that,* Sallie McFague writes, and if enough of us think like that—if enough of us live like that—then reality will become more like we believe it to be. That is not a vicious circle, but a hope against hope. We can create reality—in fact, we do so all the time.

Look around. The world is going to pieces, but we are so used to the destruction going on around us—the fumes, the open landfills, the disappearance of trees, the dead possums and raccoons and fox and red-tailed hawks on the side of the road—that we don't see the emergency. Ecological deterioration is more like drug addiction than war: It creeps up on us daily while we deny everything. We are dealing with a wily, crafty enemy: ourselves.

Body is the model I suggest for God—and not just the human body. But the body of a mountain. Heavenly bodies. Oceanic bodies. The atoms in our bodies were formed in the bodies of the early stars.

Here is my wager: That we love and honor bodies—our bodies, the bodies of others, the bodies of all life forms on the planet. That we see the body not as a discardable garment but as the shape of who we are. That we understand salvation not as escaping the body, but as the well-being of the body.

Isn't that the primary belief of Christianity? Isn't the doctrine of the incarnation the belief that God is with us, here, on earth? Stretch that beyond Jesus to include all matter. Stretch and believe God is incarnated in the world. Believe our planet—even the entire universe—is the body of God.

Eric was hired by a university in Southern California, so we moved further west. I wrote my dissertation on the Abu Ghraib photographs and taught part-time at the university where Eric worked. I spent the mornings reading government memos sanctioning torture, going through transcripts of interviews with people who had been tortured, looking at photographs of people in pain, and then, at noon, on the days I wasn't teaching, I walked downstairs, turned on the television, and watched the makeover show *What Not to Wear.* I kept the volume low. I slunk down on the couch so no one could see me. I didn't answer the phone.

The show was always the same: An unsuspecting person is nominated by her friends and family for a makeover. Hidden cameras film her at work, on the street, out with friends, in her home. The hosts of the show, Stacy and Clinton, surprise her and demand she hand herself—body, mind, wardrobe—over to them in exchange for a five-thousand-dollar shopping spree. She flies to New York City. She shops. She resists. She gets frustrated. Stacy and Clinton help her. She gets a haircut. She has her makeup done. She is made new. Her friends and family throw a party. They sip cocktails. She makes an entrance. She spins around. People clap and cheer. I always cried at this part of the show, at just how *happy* everyone is, at what a *relief* it is to have her internal beauty on the outside so everyone can see it, at how much everyone *loves* her. *Watch me, love me, save me,* I thought, sitting on the couch.

I wanted to be friends with Stacy and Clinton. Even more, I wanted them to come get me for a makeover. I spent most days writing in pajamas—capri-length sweatpants (Stacy and Clinton hate sweatpants worn outside the gym), a fleece hoodie (Stacy and Clinton hate fleece and hoodies), and slippers ("Have you given up?" they ask guests with this shoe preference). Although I was the perfect candidate, they never came to my door. When my doorbell did ring, I'd answer it, hopeful, but it was usually the kind deliveryman from UPS. "Are you sick again?" he asked, looking at my outfit.

At the end of the show, I wiped my eyes, turned off the television, walked back upstairs, and wrote about torture.

. . .

Eric and I were running errands after going to the farmers' market when we saw them. They stood in front of a huge sign, and the corner seemed to glow with all their brightness—yellow signs, yellow hair, white skin, white teeth. "Slow down," I said to Eric. "Slow down." I lowered the window and leaned my body as far out of the car as I could. "Bigots!" I shouted. "Bigots!" Cars piled up behind our now-stopped car, and people anxious to get to Trader Joe's or to fill their tanks with gas began to honk at us. I leaned out further. "Shame on you," I said, my finger pointing, my voice raised.

We kept driving, but they were everywhere, on every corner, as if at that very moment they were going forth and multiplying. *Vote Yes on Eight*, their signs said. *Protect traditional marriage. Protect families. Protect religious freedom. Protect our children. It's Adam and Eve, not Adam and Steve.* "What are we going to do?" I asked Eric.

In February of 2008, less than ten miles from those corners where the people against gay marriage stood, Lawrence King, a seventh grader, was shot in the head, twice, by his fourteen-year-old classmate in the computer lab at school. Lawrence told people he was gay. Sometimes he wore makeup and high heels to school.

We drove to the Democratic headquarters. Eric waited in the car, and I ran inside. "I need signs against Proposition Eight," I said to the two women at the desk. They were eating fried chicken, and they gestured toward a small table near the door. I bought twenty dollars worth of signs, and I ran back to the car. Now when we saw the yellow people, I leaned out of the window and held my dark blue sign. "No!" I shouted. "No!"

The day after Eric and I saw all the people on the corners with their yellow signs and smiling children, we attended a pro–Proposition Eight rally at a Baptist church. We carried a sign of our own. In red paint our sign said: "Remember Lawrence King? Proposition Eight sanctions THAT hate. Vote no!" We stood with our "no" sign in front of their thirty-foot "yes" sign, and a man wearing an American-flag shirt stood in front of our sign with his son. We stood on the curb, and he stood in the street. "Don't stand too close to the sodomites," he said to his son and pushed him away from us and into the street. "Faggots," he said. "Queers."

A woman holding a "yes" sign read our banner. "Oh no," she said, smiling as if it were a simple misunderstanding. "This has nothing to do with *that*. He came from a broken home." I didn't know if she meant Lawrence King or the boy who killed him.

Eric and I had agreed not to say anything to anyone, figuring our sign spoke for itself, but it was impossible to remain silent. "Haven't you read the Bible?" a woman asked us. "The Bible is very clear on this."

"I've studied the Bible for ten years," I said.

"And you're still confused?" she asked, making everyone around her laugh.

"Traditional marriage in the Bible is polygamy," I said, and when she didn't respond I asked, "Do you eat shellfish?"

"Do I eat shellfish?" she asked. "Do you hear that everyone? She doesn't even make any sense."

"Do you eat bacon?" I asked. "Do you eat rare steaks? Do you eat cheeseburgers? All of those things are prohibited in the verses that come right before the passages you people like to quote." I wanted to tell the man next to me I had my period. Leviticus also forbids men from seeing women who are menstruating.

She started moving her mouth, mocking me, making nonsense sounds. "Naa-naa-naa-naa-naa-naa," she said, sticking out her tongue. There was laughter again.

A voice came over a loudspeaker telling everyone to gather in the parking lot for prayer, and some of the laughing people left to talk to their God. The minister introduced a guest speaker, a priest from Austria. His accent was thick. "Look at what happened in Germany," he said. "They allowed gay marriage and now gay people are everywhere. You cannot avoid them. They are taking over."

"Look what happened in Germany?" I said.

"Heil Hitler," Eric said.

A woman who had not gone to pray and was still standing next to us turned to look at Eric after he spoke. "But we'll let them have civil unions," she said.

. . .

Also on the ballot that fall was Proposition Two: *Calves raised for veal, egg-laying hens, and pregnant pigs can be confined only in ways that allow these animals to lie down, stand up, fully extend their limbs, and turn around freely.* Unless you're taking them to the rodeo or fair or slaughterhouse. Then you can package them however you please.

I watched an undercover video filmed at a chicken processing plant that showed workers stomping, kicking, slamming chickens against the wall, twisting off their beaks, spitting tobacco in their eyes, spray-painting their faces. The policy at most plants is to let the birds' hearts continue to beat through slaughter. The bleed out is more efficient that way.

A bigger cage seemed a small thing, but I voted for it anyway.

Before she worked at Abu Ghraib, Lynndie England worked in a chicken processing plant, feathers in her hair.

You would like to place Zubaydah in a cramped confinement box with an insect, Assistant Attorney General Jay S. Bybee wrote in a 2002 memo to the CIA. *You have informed us that he appears to have a fear of insects. In particular, you would like to tell Zubaydah that you intend to place a stinging insect into the box with him. You would, however, place a harmless insect in the box. You have orally informed us that you would in fact place a harmless insect such as a caterpillar in the box with him.*

"Why are you a vegetarian?" a friend asked me. "And don't tell me it's for political reasons."

"Okay," I said, "I won't."

Some cages we make and some we find, some we slam shut and some we fling wide open, some we climb out of and some we climb into and pull the grate down fast, the smell of iron like blood.

. . .

I was teaching Art, Society, and Mass Media at the university and during the third week of class, I arrived early to prepare, and two of my students—a man and a woman—were already in our classroom. "Tell her," the woman said, but the man she elbowed shook his head. "Come on," she said. "Tell her." He shook his head again. "If you don't tell her, I will," she said.

"Fine," he said. "You tell her."

"He was stationed at Abu Ghraib," the student said.

I looked at him. "You were?"

"Yes," he said.

I couldn't believe it. I had spent years analyzing the photographs and researching torture, and now there was a person who had actually been at the prison. "If you ever want to talk about your time in Iraq, I'd be happy to listen," I said.

The student showed up at my office later that week. I was the first person who had asked about his time in Iraq, he said. He'd been home for three years. He told me how disorienting it was to be back, how strange he felt, out of place, alone. He missed the people he'd worked with in Iraq. He missed doing something that mattered. He missed the camaraderie. "One day we're all together," he said. "And the next day we're apart."

He told me about what happened when detainees were released from prison after it was determined they were not a threat. Each man was dressed in white and was given a small amount of cash and a Koran. "But then we kept finding their bodies outside the prison walls," he said. "They'd been robbed and decapitated. They were all wearing the same clothing, like a uniform, so it was obvious they'd just been released from an American prison, and people knew we gave them money, so we had to start dressing them in different clothes before they were released."

He told me how beautiful their prayers were, how they lay on the ground in rows, how the guards would be quiet when the prisoners prayed, and how the prisoners returned the favor by being silent on Christmas. "It was a sign of respect," he said.

He showed me bracelets children in the prison had given him. They wove them using threads from their towels, the clasp a loop over a seed from a date. "I can't get one little boy out of my mind," he said. The boy's head was flat on one side, like a deflated football. He'd been injured—by gunfire or shrapnel—and American surgeons took out part of his skull to give his swollen brain room. They put the piece of bone in between the boy's ribs to keep it part of his body while his brain recovered. But the boy was released before the swelling subsided, and in his village there are no doctors.

Once, my student helped load detainees onto cargo planes that would bring them to prison. The detainees were hooded and didn't know they were boarding a plane. He said he felt like Noah, herding animals, strapping them down like cattle. He walked each man up the plank into the dark. One urinated on himself. Another threw up. One, an old man, couldn't stop shaking. My student wanted to tell the shaking man it would be alright, but they didn't speak the same language, so he put his hand on his shoulder, gently. "I hoped my touch would communicate everything I wanted to say," he said. In the air, the detainees moved their mouths to release the pressure in their ears, and the soldiers laughed nervously. They didn't know what else to do.

My student lived for a year in a prison cell. Wind came through the hole blown through one of the walls. The first few nights at Abu Ghraib the soldiers had nothing—no blankets, no beds. He covered himself with magazines to keep warm. "I felt like a prisoner," he said. "I slept in a cell. I couldn't go home." When the detainees asked him where he was from, where he lived, he always said, "I live in Abu Ghraib."

The soldier in my class thought his ribs were broken. He thought his heart was breaking. He thought he might be dying. He went to the VA hospital. He saw a doctor. He had an EKG. They took X-rays of his chest. The doctor showed him the images. *It's not your ribs. It's not your heart,* she said. *It's your head.*

"If it's just my head," he told me during my office hours, "I don't need to go back to the doctor."

When Moses comes down the mountain holding the tablets after seeing what no human being should see, the skin of his face is shining. With a veil, Moses covers his face.

. . .

I wish I'd lost my faith. Put it in a place I can't remember. Looked away when it wandered off. I wish my faith had disappeared like music. Analog to digital. Vinyl to disc to MP3. Waves compressed. Instruments dropped, beats missed, distortion. An untrained ear can't tell the difference. Most of the college students I teach now have never heard a record, don't know the grooves' secrets, the static sound that silence makes—but they listen to music all the time.

I didn't lose my faith, I left it. It's all still there. I know right where it is. I can see it through that window stained with story—see the pews and altar, see the vestments, see the books, see the kneeling, praying, eating, breaking, loving, blessing, forgiving, bleeding, redeeming. But I can't make myself go inside.

My mind is like a record, grooved, depressed, canyoned, but its needle won't play that music anymore, no matter how hard I force it down.

God is gone—but not completely. When I close my eyes I still see a bearded white man. A decade of study can't wipe him out. I feel him there, hovering. But that version of God has become ethically untenable for me. Too many terrible things done in his name. Too much suffering in the world. Too much violence. Too many disasters. I let go of a personal God. I let go of all of it.

When I tell people I can't be a priest and I can't be Christian and I can't go to church and I can't believe in an omnipotent God or a benevolent God or a God who is a being or who has a will or who is watching over the world, they usually say, *But God doesn't cause the violence in the world.* They are talking about theodicy, the various solutions architected to show how it's possible to have an all-powerful good God and still have so much pain and suffering in the world. They are talking about free will and the afterlife and a God who doesn't cause suffering but is present when we suffer. They are talking about a God who is "the companion of sufferers."

And I see the allure. It can be lonely out here.

. . .

I don't go to church, but I do go to the covered stalls of the farmers' market on Saturday mornings—wildflower honey, olive oil, butter lettuce, collard greens, arugula, Swiss chard, beets, snap peas, artichokes, fava beans, *haricots verts,* strawberries, peaches, oranges, orchids, ranunculus, butternut squash, avocados, heirloom tomatoes, lemons, lavender, basil, thyme—a place in which I can believe. I buy eggs from Varden, a farmer from Nipomo who wears overalls and shows me pictures of hens—*my girls,* he calls them—and they are not in cages. He talks about his girlfriend, lends me books about soil, makes compost tea, and asks, every week, *What's for show and tell?* At home I crack shells so thick they clog the disposal. I keep them in a bin with other vegetable scraps we blend in our food processor and give to the worms we keep in the three-tray black plastic bin on our front porch.

This is a kind of faith for me. To be in season. To crave what the earth makes when the time is right. To know who grows my food and how they grow it. To know that it has not been sprayed or injected or genetically modified or fertilized with toxic chemicals. To know who picks it and what they are paid and what their working conditions are like. To thank the farmers who planted and tended and harvested and brought it to market.

Yet even as I write that, a voice in my head says, *Really? You're going to end your book about God with the farmers' market?*

Yes. I'm going to end my book about God with the farmers' market.

It is a small thing.

And it is not a small thing.

If I can't say no to the suffering caused by what I choose to feed myself, by what I have a taste for, then what can I say no to?

Food is what most religions have in common. Shared meals. Taboos. Dietary restrictions. Rules. Fasting. Rituals for blessing, serving, eating. It used to be that what mattered in the Eucharist was not the consecration, not the altar cloths, not the priest—what mattered was receiving the bread and wine in community. Making sure the people around you were nourished. Break. Receive. Give.

Communion is not about making one meal sacred on one morning in one holy space, but about making all meals, all eating, all feeding sacred. If the Sunday bread and wine matter, then all bread and all wine matter, then all eating matters—and if all eating matters, then it matters that we create a world in which everyone has enough to eat.

But almost one billion people are hungry. And it is estimated that twenty-four thousand children die every day from hunger and poverty and preventable diseases and illnesses.

And on my plate today there is a sliced ripe tomato, just picked, still sun warm.

What if there is no grand narrative? What if there is only the meaning found in everyday ethics, in trying to live with integrity, in the messy, nebulous, complicated work of caring for what's around you—and for what's not—in trying not to harm another living being?

There is no innocent space, I know. I know I am a hypocrite, complicit. I know my country is sending drones, dropping bombs, inscribing biblical verses on the scopes of our soldiers' guns, John 8:12—*I am the light of the world. Whoever follows me will never walk in darkness but will have the light of life.*

What if this is all there is?

I used to sit on my deck in Idaho and watch the summer sunset, the sky turn pink, cerulean, midnight blue, the mountain go dark in silhouette, and I'd think about God.

Now I think about the sunset. Now I look around.

In my search for God, I missed the world right here. Aspen. Lupine. Big Wood River. Red-winged blackbird. Elk. Mountain bluebird. Magpie. Sage.

In a poem by Marie Howe called "The Gate," the narrator's brother who is dying says, *This is what you have been waiting for.*

What? the narrator asks.

This, he says, holding up her cheese and mustard sandwich.

What? the narrator asks again.

This, he says, sort of looking around.

On a trip to Kings Canyon one summer, Eric took me on a hike to see a waterfall. *It looks like a cathedral,* was my first thought, and then, *No, a cathedral looks like this.*

. . .

On an episode of *This American Life* called "Superpowers," John Hodgman asks people this question: Flight or invisibility? Whichever you pick, he says, you will be the only person in the world to have that particular superpower. You can't have both. You have to choose.

I listened as people explained their choices to Hodgman. Those who selected invisibility talked about their desires to sneak into movies for free, to stow away undetected on airplanes, to listen to people talk about you when they think you're not there, to watch people when they can't see you (especially when they're naked), to steal. They wanted to be able to do what they would never allow themselves to do otherwise, and they wanted to get away with it. Those who chose flight simply wanted to be able to travel to places more easily—bars, doctors' offices, Atlantic

City, Paris. They wanted to avoid taking the bus. Although the people Hodgman interviewed seemed to think of themselves as superheroes once they were granted flight or invisibility, none of them described anything generous or justice-oriented that they'd do with their special power. They were not the crime-fighting kind of superhero, they explained, because a single superpower was simply inadequate to make that kind of work possible. They reasoned they'd need other superpowers—a package of superpowers in fact—to be able to do good.

Many of the people interviewed argued that your answer to the question about flight or invisibility reveals something about the kind of person you are. One woman—who chose invisibility—said the choice is connected to a person's level of shame. Do you have nothing to hide or do you want to hide yourself? Are you a person who flies or are you a person who fades? For Hodgman, the real questions underlying the choice between flight and invisibility are these: Who do you want to be? The person you hope to be? Or the person you actually fear that you are?

But for me, the subjects' answers exposed something else: We don't really want to be the person who could save the world. Even if we're invisible. Even if we can fly. We want it to be someone else.

And didn't my ideas about God say something similar?

The theologian Ludwig Feuerbach argues in his book *The Essence of Christianity* that Christianity has taken everything that is good about humanity and projected it onto God. All of the good things that belong to us as a species—love, generosity, strength, beauty, justice—we've given to God. God and humans have been mistakenly constructed as opposites: God infinite, humans finite; God perfect, humans imperfect; God eternal, humans temporal; God almighty, humans weak; God holy, humans sinful. The good news, however, at least according to Feuerbach, is that this situation can be easily remedied. All we need to recognize is that the qualities we have ascribed to God actually belong to humanity.

In other words, Christianity has turned God into a kind of superhero capable of doing everything human beings can't do, a move that renders humans helpless, small, in need of rescue. We enrich God, Feuerbach argues, but we impoverish the world.

We know what will save us. We see it. Paint it. Build it. Think it. Dream it. Imagine it. But then we call it God. *That does not belong to me,* we say. *I could never be like that.*

But what if it does belong to you? What if humanity has alienated itself from what is ours? "I am not saying God is nothing, the Trinity is nothing, the Word of God is nothing," Feuerbach writes. "I only show that they are not the illusions that theology makes them—they are not foreign, but native mysteries, the mysteries of human nature." When I read Feuerbach, I hear Sweet Honey in the Rock singing the words to one of June Jordan's poems: *We are the ones we have been waiting for.*

An Anthropologist's God

When a bird imagines God, God is winged. When a plant imagines God, God is rooted and blooming. When a sun imagines God, God burns.

Ludwig Feuerbach called his book *The Essence of Christianity,* but he wanted to call it *Know Thyself.* In that book he writes, you imagine the best version of yourself, but then you pretend it doesn't belong to you, and you name it God. Christianity alienated human beings from what is theirs. All that's good it gave away.

But what you think of as united, you unite. What you think of as distinct, you separate. What you think of as destroyed, you destroy. What you think of as loved, you love.

Can you see? You can save your life. You can save others' lives.

Imagine a screen. Project goodness. Project strength. Project holiness. Kindness. Mercy. Love. Watch the screen. Long for what it shows. Bow down. Worship.

Now imagine a mirror. See goodness. See strength. See holiness. Kindness. Mercy. Love. See they belong to us.

I'm not post-God. I'm just through thinking about God as a being. If God is mystery, if God is more than anything we can say or think or believe about God, then I am agnostic. "Maybe the less we know, the more faithful we are," Gordon Kaufman said to my friend Katie Ford.

This is what I believe in: Mystery. Agency. Creativity. Justice. Accountability. Love.

This is my faith: a fragile hope in what humanity might be able to do when we stop looking for someone else to save us.

The Mayan people of Acteal live in a village in Chiapas, Mexico. They call themselves *Las Abejas*—the Bees—because they work together. They are Catholic pacifists believing that is the way to follow Jesus. One Sunday morning in December of 1997 they were praying for peace in their chapel and were attacked by armed men. The men were Protestants and had attended their own churches that very morning.

Forty-five *Abejas* were killed. Thirty-six women and children. Nine men. Twenty-six people were wounded.

They buried the bodies in the floor of the chapel.

The Mexican government considered these peasant pacifists dangerous. After the massacre, the government built an army post beside the entrance to Acteal. When the women left their community, the soldiers stationed there threatened to rape them. *We will wipe you out*, the soldiers said.

Las Abejas knew what to do. They found a spool of green thread, and they walked the perimeter of their village, circling it with thread. Unarmed, they stood by the green thread day and night and respectfully asked armed people not to cross it.

. . .

People are wrapping the world in thread.

. . .

Denis Mukwege, a doctor in eastern Congo, said in 2007 that ten new women and girls who had been raped showed up at his hospital every day, torn open by bayonets and razor blades and chunks of wood, their reproductive and digestive systems damaged beyond repair. Gangs of men arrive in villages and butcher the people they find there. They kidnap women, tie them to trees, release them only to gang-rape them, and tie the women up again when they are through. The attacks continued despite the presence of the largest United Nations peacekeeping force in the world, more than seventeen thousand troops.

The peacekeepers began what they called "night flashes." Three truckloads of peacekeepers drive into the bush and keep their headlights on all night. The light lets civilians and armed groups know the peacekeepers are present. "Sometimes," the *New York Times* reported, "when morning comes, three thousand villagers are curled up on the ground around them." Trying to get inside that light.

. . .

People are keeping their lights on all night.

. . .

In 1977, Carl Sagan was asked by NASA to compile a mix tape of the human experience, a recording of the sounds that reflect human life on this planet. Those sounds would be made into gold records, that would be placed in two capsules, which would be shot into space, moving at an average speed of thirty-five thousand miles per hour for the next billion years with the hope that somehow, millions of years from now, an alien will find the capsule, find a way to play the record, and discover what life was like for human beings on planet Earth.

Sagan appointed Annie Druyan as the creative director of the Voyager Interstellar Record project, and while they were working together, they fell madly in love.

On the album they included the sound of a kiss, a mother's first words to her newborn baby, Mozart, Bach, Beethoven, a twenty-five hundred-year-old-piece of Chinese music called "Flowing Streams," greetings in fifty-five human languages, the greetings of the humpback whales. "It was a sacred undertaking," Druyan said. "Because it was saying, we want to be citizens of the cosmos. We want you to know about us."

They also decided to measure the electrical impulses of a human brain and nervous system, turn the data into sound, and put it on the record. Maybe, they thought, whoever finds the record in the future will be able to reconstitute that data into thought. They recorded the sounds of Druyan in meditation two days after she and Sagan declared their love for each other. She meditated about the wonder of love. Her brain waves, heartbeat, eyes in REM, every little sound her body was making—the sounds of a body in love.

Sagan and Druyan were together for twenty years until Sagan's death in 1996. Even now, when she's down, she thinks of those two spacecraft. "And still they move at thirty-five thousand miles per hour," she said, "leaving our solar system for the great wide-open sea of interstellar space."

. . .

People are sending the sounds of love into space.

. . .

Some people live on top of mountains in glass houses watching over forests, looking for smoke. One man has spent more than twenty summers in a fourteen-square-foot cabin on top of Saddleback Mountain in California minding a piece of the Tahoe National Forest. His version of paradise. He has four pairs of binoculars, cameras. He knows the landscape so well, he says, that it's easy to see when something's amiss.

That is how I used to imagine God: high in the sky looking after me, making sure I didn't burn up or disappear or feel too alone. What comfort came with this belief. And what loss when I decided God was not in that house with the 360-degree view.

I thought that meant no one was in the house.

In most of the gospel stories, Jesus keeps saying beautiful, poetic, profound things to his disciples, and they keep not getting it. They don't even spend time reflecting. They just ask the same questions over and over again. In the Gospel of Thomas, Jesus tells his disciples that they have come from light, that they are children of light, that God is in them. He says, *If they ask you 'What is the evidence of your God in you?' say to them 'It is motion and rest,'* and you can almost hear the disciples' disappointment. They are not satisfied being divine children of light. They want to know what will happen when they die. When the world will be better than it is. What to stake their lives on. Enough with grapevines and wineskins and treasure buried in fields. Enough with mustard seeds and yeast and nets thrown into the sea. Tell us the truth.

So they ask again: When will the new world come?

What you look for has come, but you do not know it.

And again: When will the new world come?

It will not come by watching for it.

And again: When will anything be different?

It already is.

When will there be no pain?

Fill the jars with water.

When will we have new life?

Your lamp is under a basket. Your lamp is under your bed.

Do you not care that we are perishing?

Let anyone with ears to hear listen.

Who are you to say these things?

Show me the stone the builders rejected. It is the cornerstone.

How should we pray?

Split a piece of wood. I am there.

Who can be saved?

Find a colt that has never been ridden. Untie it.

By what authority do you do these things?
You are not far from it.
Are you the Messiah?
As the branches become tender, you know summer is near.
Have you no answer?
Keep awake.
Again they ask: When will the new world come?
And again he answers: *It is spread out on the earth. You do not see it.*

Someone is on top of that mountain in that glass house watching over the world. Sometimes it's you, and sometimes it's me. The only ones watching for smoke, the only ones ready to sound the alarm, the only ones who will bring water, are the people down here with us. Just us, looking after each other.

POSTSCRIPT

ARE YOU STILL CHRISTIAN? people ask, and I'm not sure what to say. Do I go to church? No. Do I believe God is a Trinity? No. Do I still know by heart the words to creeds, to hymns, to prayers? Yes. Do I follow Jesus's teachings? Yes, some of them, depending on the translation. Do I believe Jesus was the Son of God? I don't even know what that question means.

Sometimes I say, *Yes, I'm Christian*, because I want those words to belong to me. I don't want to give up the religion I've spent most of my life believing. I don't want to cede that territory to the other people waiting to claim it. I want to speak with authority, and authority is not often granted to outsiders, no matter how much they know.

But more often now I say, *No, I'm not Christian*. The first time I said those words out loud I looked around, felt my face get hot, braced myself. It's frightening to put yourself on the other side of salvation.

. . .

After I say *I'm not Christian*, some people ask, *But you still believe in God, right?* The truthful answer is *I don't know.* Sometimes I imagine the God I broke up with laughing at me, a mean laugh, belittling. *You'll see*, I hear him say. *You'll see.* Other times I imagine him waiting patiently for me to figure out he's the one, arms folded on his chest, head cocked to one side, giving me space to find my own way, wanting the best for me, no matter what that might mean for us.

When you break up with someone, it doesn't mean he ceases to exist. You bump into each other around town. You talk about meeting for coffee. You see your love with other people, and it makes you jealous, makes you consider getting back together, makes you wonder if you made a mistake when you called it quits. The version of God I used to love is still out there in the world, hanging around in churches, showing up in people's prayers and hearts and imaginations, playing his role in the stories we like to tell. But I know he's not the right God for me. I try to remember that.

. . .

When the disciples discovered they had followed someone who turned out not to be who they believed him to be, when events did not go as they planned, when their grief was terrible, their fear so intense they locked themselves in that upper room, they wrote about it.

Love one another.

I walked away from Christianity and left behind the story I had been telling about my life, the story in which I needed God to feel right, seen, loved, safe, chosen. Without that version of God, I had to write something new.

Words are world-making—they get inside our heads and shape the stories we tell about what is possible—for ourselves, for the earth, for all the beings we share this earth with. God says, *Let there be light,* and there is light. To make something beautiful—a painting, a novel, a sculpture, a meal, a play—is world-changing. *Look!* I imagine these creations saying. *The whole world is a sanctuary. Look! We can make the world a place where everyone and everything can thrive.*

Christianity made a world for me to inhabit. Heaven above. Hell below. The earth God's creation. My self knit by God in my mother's womb, every hair on my head counted, every thought in my head known. Commandments. Rules. Sin. Salvation. Eternal life. I believed that world was all there was. How could I leave when I thought there was nowhere else to go?

When Eric was in fourth grade, his parents took him to Sunday school at a Lutheran Church, and after they dropped him off, the pastor's wife pulled Eric aside.

The other children were eating cookies on the far side of the room, but she handed him a flashlight and a piece of paper with the Lord's Prayer written on it. She led him to a cardboard refrigerator box and told him he couldn't come out until he knew the prayer by heart. He climbed inside. She closed the lid.

I didn't have to crawl inside the refrigerator box offered to me, but I did. I spent years sitting in the darkness clinging to the small light they gave me, playing by their rules and saying the words they wanted me to say and being the person they wanted me to be so that someday they might think I was good enough for them to let me out. I grew afraid to leave the box because it started to feel safe, because it almost felt like home, but then I remembered this: There was a whole world out there waiting for me. I was free to go. I always had been.

NOTES

PROLOGUE

(Pg vii) **Love after Love:** "Love after Love" from *Collected Poems* 1948–1984 by Derek Walcott. Copyright © 1986 by Derek Walcott. Reprinted by permission of Farrar, Straus and Giroux, LLC.

(Pg 7) **My friend Maylen told me a story she heard about a bird trap in India:** This is Maylen Dominguez's version of a story that Paramahamsa Nithyananda tells.

1. FROM AFAR

(Pg 26) ***Stigma*, the brand burned on an animal**: http://www.gospel-mysteries.net/stigmata.html and http://www.newadvent.org/cathen/14294b.htm

(Pg 33) **A Mystic's God:** Julian of Norwich, *Revelations of Divine Love* (New York: Penguin, 1998), 7 and Margery Kempe, *The Book of Margery Kempe* (New York: Penguin, 1985), 41–42.

2. THE ART OF LOVE

(Pg 52) **Note that, in this bitterness, delight:** This stanza is from the Wallace Stevens poem "The Poems of Our Climate," which can be found on page 143 of the book *Wallace Stevens: The Poems of Our Climate,* by Harold Bloom, published in 1980 and used here by permission of the publisher, Cornell University Press.

(Pg 56) **She could see it all so clearly:** Virginia Woolf, *To the Lighthouse* (New York: Harcourt Brace Jovanovich, 1981), 19. Excerpt from *To the Lighthouse* by Virginia Woolf, copyright 1927 by Harcourt, Inc. and renewed 1954 by Leonard Woolf. Reprinted by permission of Houghton Mifflin Harcourt Publishing Company.

(Pg 57) **Woolf writes that even Jane Austen didn't have a room of her own:** Virginia Woolf, *A Room of One's Own* (New York: Harcourt Brace & Company, 1989), 67. Woolf quotes a memoir written by Austen's nephew: "She had no separate study to repair to, and most of the work must have been done in the general sitting-room, subject to all kinds of casual interruptions."

(Pg 62) **I took The Phenomenology of Religion my senior year**: The descriptions I have written about what happened during the lectures Dupré gave are based on my memory and the notes I took in the spring semester of 1995 in his class at Yale University, Religious Studies 4317, Phenomenology of Religion. Some passages are also taken from his book: Louis K. Dupré, *The Other Dimension: A Search for the Meaning of Religious Studies* (New York: Doubleday, 1972).

(Pg 63) **Then he answered his question with a love story:** Dupré is using the philosopher Meister Eckhart to tell this story.

3. GOD + SARAH = LOVE

(Pg 68) **My group's mentor was twenty-two years old:** I wrote about the phonics routine in my first book: *Taught By America: A Story of Struggle and Hope in Compton* (Boston, Mass: Beacon Press, 2005).

(Pg 74) **One of my friend's seventh-grade students:** I wrote about my friend's student in *Taught by America*.

(Pg 75) **James Cone's God:** I constructed this passage using direct quotations from Cone's *A Black Theology of Liberation* and my own words inspired by Cone. Please see: James H. Cone, *A Black Theology of Liberation* (Maryknoll: Orbis, 1994). Used by permission of Orbis Books.

(Pg 78) **In *On Beauty and Being Just*, Elaine Scarry uses a poem by Emily Dickinson:** Elaine Scarry, *On Beauty and Being Just* (Princeton: Princeton University Press, 1999), 12. The poem was reprinted here by permission of the publishers and the Trustees of Amherst College from *The Poems of Emily Dickinson: Variorum Edition,* edited by Ralph W. Franklin, Cambridge, Mass.: The Belknap Press of Harvard University Press, Copyright © 1951, 1955, 1979, 1983 by the President and Fellows of Harvard College.

(Pg 83) **God didn't become human to prove how wretched we are:** I heard this from Tim Safford in 1997 at All Saints Episcopal Church in Pasadena.

(Pg 83) **The power of the resurrection:** This paragraph is based on a talk given by Gary Hall at a Covenant II meeting in 1997 at All Saints Episcopal Church in Pasadena.

(Pg 83) **Desmond Tutu's God:** This passage is based on a speech I heard Archbishop Tutu give at the Episcopal Divinity School in Cambridge.

(Pg 87) **A Romantic's God:** I constructed this passage using direct quotations from Schleiermacher's *On Religion* and *The Christian Faith*, as well as my own words and notes from lectures I heard David Lamberth give on Schleiermacher in the many theology courses I took from him at Harvard Divinity School between 1998 and 2001. For more information, please see: Friedrich Schleiermacher, *On Religion: Speeches to Its Cultured Despisers* (Cambridge; New York: Cambridge University Press, 1996), and Friedrich Schleiermacher, *The Christian Faith* (Edinburgh: T&T Clark, 1989), 12.

(Pg 88) **Cameron believes we are victims of our own internalized perfectionist**: Julia Cameron, *The Artist's Way: A Spiritual Path to Higher Creativity* (New York: Putnam, 1992), 11.

(Pg 89) **I once heard that to try to understand what their patients with schizophrenia experience**: "The Sights and Sounds of Schizophrenia," Joanne Silberner, NPR, August 29, 2002. The program can be listened to and downloaded at: http://www.npr.org/programs/atc/features/2002/aug/schizophrenia/

(Pg 90) **I went to a workshop on prayer at All Saints:** The words I give to Anne Peterson here are from a Covenant II class that I took at All Saints Episcopal Church in the spring of 1997. Peterson was the leader of the class on prayer, and some of her words here are her own, and some are words she shared with us from a handout of quotations about prayer. One of these quotations was from another priest at the church, Clarke Oler, who begins his course Spiritual Direction: Practicing the Presence of God with these comments: "The experience of prayer is diametrically opposed to what our world teaches us to expect: quick results from hard work . . . we [need not] learn to pray harder, but how to relax and let God come closer; not how to achieve the love of God by prayer and concentration, but, how to respond to the love of God that is already being offered to us; not how to be more dutiful, but how to be more faithful in a love relationship. Our goal in prayer is to learn to be more open to receive the loving care of the indwelling God."

(Pg 92) **One Sunday Ed Bacon gave a sermon on vocation**: Ed Bacon, January 29, 1996, All Saints Episcopal Church.

(Pg 95) **Communion is anti-amnesia:** This description is taken from a handout about Communion given to me by Clarke Oler that included a quotation by Kenneth Leech. The quotation can be found in the first chapter of Leech's *We Preach Christ Crucified*.

4. MOVING IN TOGETHER

(Pg 110) **The seminar I took with Gordon Kaufman:** The ideas and words that I attribute to Kaufman come from my conversations with him, the classes I took with him, and his books. For more information, please see: Gordon D. Kaufman, *An Essay on Theological Method* (Atlanta: Scholars Press, 1995), 7; Gordon D. Kaufman, "My Life and My Theological Reflection: Two Central Themes," *American Journal of Theology and Philosophy* Vol. 22, No. 1, January 2001 (2001): 3–32; Gordon D. Kaufman, "On Thinking of God as Serendipitous Creativity," *Journal of the American Academy of Religion* 69, No. 2 (2001): 409–25; Gordon D. Kaufman, *In the Beginning: Creativity* (Minneapolis, MN: Fortress Press, 2004); and Gordon D. Kaufman, *In Face of Mystery: A Constructive Theology* (Cambridge: Harvard University Press, 1993).

(Pg 115) **In his book *In Face of Mystery*, Kaufman quotes the Jewish philosopher Martin Buber**: On pages 5–6 of *In Face of Mystery*, Kaufman is quoting Martin Buber. The passage quoted by Kaufman originally appeared in the following: Buber, Martin, *Eclipse of God* (New York: Humanity Books, 1998), 7–8. Used by permission of the Estate of Marin Buber.

(Pg 118) **Gordon Kaufman's God:** I wrote this passage using direct quotations from Kaufman's texts, my own words, and pieces of conversations I have had with Kaufman. For more information, please see: Gordon D. Kaufman, *An Essay on Theological Method*, 41; Gordon D. Kaufman, "In the Beginning . . . Creativity," (2002), 106; and Gordon D. Kaufman, *The Theological Imagination: Constructing the Concept of God* (Philadelphia: The Westminster Press, 1981), 155–56. Used by permission of Augsburg Fortress Publishers.

(Pg 119) **In 1945 an Egyptian farmer:** Karen L. King, *What is Gnosticism?* (Cambridge: Belknap Press of Harvard University Press, 2003); and Elaine H. Pagels, *The Gnostic Gospels* (New York: Random House, 1979).

(Pg 119) **In these manuscripts were sayings of Jesus:** James McConkey Robinson, and Richard Smith, *The Nag Hammadi Library in English* (San Francisco: Harper & Row, 1988), 126.

(Pg 120) **There were arguments that Jesus's teachings:** Karen L. King, *What is Gnosticism?*, 1, 3- 4.

(Pg 120) **In the *Gospel of Mary*, Peter says to Mary:** Karen L. King, *The Gospel of Mary of Magdala: Jesus and the First Woman Apostle* (Santa Rosa: Polebridge Press, 2003).

(Pg 122) **But the history of Christianity is nothing like that:** I learned this in classes I took at Harvard Divinity School with Karen King between 1998 and 2001.

(Pg 123) **Christianity has long been manipulated:** Mary Daly, *Beyond God the Father: Toward a Philosophy of Women's Liberation* (Boston: Beacon Press, 1985), 3.

(Pg 124) **Slavery must be in line with God's will:** Katie G. Cannon, *Katie's Canon: Womanism and the Soul of the Black Community* (New York: Continuum, 1995), 43–45; and James H. Cone, *Black Theology and Black Power* (Maryknoll: Orbis Books, 1997).

(Pg 124) **One of my professors, Elisabeth Schüssler Fiorenza:** Elisabeth Schüssler Fiorenza, *Bread Not Stone: The Challenge of Feminist Biblical Interpretation* (Boston: Beacon Press, 1995); and Elisabeth Schüssler Fiorenza, *In Memory of Her: A Feminist Theological Reconstruction of Christian Origins* (New York: Crossroad, 1994).

(Pg 125) **Tertullian defines women as the devil's gateway:** Mary Daly, *Beyond God the Father,* 3–4, 8.

(Pg 125) **Elizabeth Cady Stanton, a nineteenth-century proponent of women's rights:** Elizabeth Cady Stanton, *The Original Feminist Attack on the Bible (the Woman's Bible)* (New York: Arno Press, 1974), 8.

(Pg 126) **What does it do to a little girl to grow up being told she is not made in the image of God:** Carol P. Christ, *Rebirth of the Goddess: Finding Meaning in Feminist Spirituality* (Reading: Addison-Wesley, 1997), 2.

(Pg 128) **Mary Daly's God:** I wrote this passage using direct quotes from Mary Daly's books and my own words. For more information, please see the following: Mary Daly, *Beyond God the Father,* 69; and Mary Daly and Jane Caputi, *Webster's First New Intergalactic Wickedary of the English Language* (San Francisco: Harper

Collins, 1987). Copyright © 1973, 1985 by Mary Daly. Reprinted by permission of Beacon Press, Boston.

(Pg 132) ***Listen to this,* God said:** Elaine H. Pagels, *The Gnostic Gospels*, xv. Pagels is quoting the *Gospel of Thomas*.

(Pg 135) **A Philosopher's God:** Alfred North Whitehead, *Process 133 Reality, an Essay in Cosmology* (Cambridge: University Press, 1929), 346.

5. WHO ARE YOU AND WHY ARE YOU IN MY HOUSE?

(Pg 148) **"Do you see this rock?":** I wrote a version of this story in *A Church of Her Own*. Please see: Sarah Sentilles, *A Church of Her Own: What Happens When a Woman Takes the Pulpit* (Orlando: Harcourt, 2008).

(Pg 150) **A Theologian's God:** I wrote this passage using direct quotes from Paul Tillich's texts and my own words. Please see: Paul Tillich, *Systematic Theology* (Chicago: University of Chicago Press, 1951), 211; Paul Tillich, *Dynamics of Faith* (New York: Harper, 1958), 31; and Paul Tillich, *Theology of Culture* (New York: Oxford University Press, 1959), 10.

(Pg 153) **I heard a story on the radio about a woman who came home from work:** RADIOLAB, "Do I Know You?" March 8, 2010. You can listen to and download the podcast here: http://www.radiolab.org/blogs/radiolab-blog/2010/mar/08/do-i-know-you/

(Pg 171) **I was also part of a small group of women:** I describe my ordination in *A Church of Her Own*.

(Pg 177) **Rainer Maria Rilke's God:** I first heard this Rilke poem on the radio program *Speaking of Faith* hosted by Krista Tippet (now called *Being*). : "ich liebe dich, du sanftestes. . . /I love you, gentlest of Ways," from *Rilke's Book of Hours: Love Poems to God* by Rainer Maria Rilke, translated by Anita Barrows and Joanna Macy, copyright © 1996 by Anita Barrows and Joanna Macy. Used by permission of Riverhead Books, an imprint of Penguin Group (USA) Inc.

(Pg 178) **Terry Tempest Williams writes that when you first encounter Utah's deserts:** Terry Tempest Williams, *Red: Passion and Patience in the Desert* (New York: Vintage Books, 2002).

(Pg 179) **Each of us "carries a tender spot:** Naomi Shihab Nye, "Jerusalem," in *Red Suitcase* (Brockport: BOA Editions, 1994), 21.

6. SEEING OTHER PEOPLE

(Pg 183) **If humans are the animals who believe:** Mark Rowlands, *The Philosopher and the Wolf: Lessons from the Wild on Love, Death, and Happiness* (London: Granta, 2008), 2.

(Pg 184) **They say the brain is like a railroad:** http://www.alz.org/index.asp

(Pg 185) **Scientists recently studied the brains of Buddhist monks:** I heard about this study on *Speaking of Faith* (now called *Being*) during the show "The 'Happiest' Man in the World," which was first broadcast on November 12, 2009. You can listen to and download the show here: http://being.publicradio.org/programs/2009/ricard/

(Pg 186) **Scientists attached electrodes to the monk's skull:** Jake Wallis Simons, "The Happiest Men in the World." *The Times*. February 8, 2010. Viewed on June 22, 2010 at http://www.timesonline.co.uk/tol/life_and_style/health/features/article7016914.ece

(Pg 188) **There's a story I heard about a woman who's starving:** This is a retelling of a story I read in Don Miguel Ruiz's book *The Mastery of Love* in a chapter called "The Magical Kitchen." Please see: Miguel Ruiz, *The Mastery of Love: A Practical Guide to the Art of Relationship* (San Rafael: Amber-Allen Pub, 1999).

(Pg 195) **An American's God:** I wrote this section using the transcript of the deposition given by Ameen Sa'eed Al-Sheikh found in Mark Danner's *Torture and Truth*. Please see: Mark Danner, "The Depositions: The Prisoners Speak, " in *Torture and Truth: America, Abu Ghraib, and the War on Terror* (New York: New York Review of Books, 2004), 226.

(Pg 200) **In Idaho I read Michael Pollan's *The Omnivore's Dilemma*:** Michael Pollan, *The Omnivore's Dilemma: A Natural History of Four Meals* (New York: Penguin Press, 2006), 113–14.

(Pg 202) **An Ecologist's God:** I wrote this passage using direct quotes from Sallie McFague's *The Body of God* and my own words. Please see: Sallie McFague, *The Body of God: An Ecological Theology* (Minneapolis: Fortress Press, 1993), xi. Used by permission of Augsburg Fortress Publishers.

(Pg 209) **I watched an undercover video:** For more information, please visit http://www.utilitarian.net/singer/by/20040725.htm and http://www.peta.org/tv/videos/graphic/326116182001.aspx

(Pg 209) **Before she worked at Abu Ghraib:** http://www.usatoday.com/news/world/iraq/2004-05-06-soldiers-usat_x.htm

(Pg 209) ***You would like to place Zubaydah in a cramped confinement box with an insect*:** Jay S. Bybee, "Memorandum for John Rizzo, Acting General Counsel of the Central Intelligence Agency," (2002), 3.

(Pg 214) **"the companion of sufferers":** James H. Cone, *The Spirituals and the Blues: An Interpretation* (Maryknoll: Orbis Books, 1991), 58.

(Pg 216) **It used to be that what mattered:** I learned this at All Saints Episcopal Church in Pasadena from Tim Safford on May 18, 1997.

(Pg 216) **But almost one billion people are hungry:** http://www.bread.org/hunger/global/ and http://www.worldhunger.org/articles/Learn/world%20hunger%20facts%202002.htm and http://www.globalissues.org/article/715/today-over–24000-children-died-around-the-world

(Pg 217) **inscribing biblical verses on the scopes of our soldiers' guns:** Joseph Rhee, Tahman Bradley, and Brian Ross, "U.S. Military Weapons Inscribed with Secret 'Jesus' Bible Codes," abcnews.com, January 18, 2010. Downloaded from http://abcnews.go.com/Blotter/us-military-weapons-inscribed-secret-jesus-bible-codes/story?id=9575794 on August 26, 2010.

(Pg 217) **In a poem by Marie Howe called "The Gate":** Marie 215, "The Gate" from Roger Housden, ed. *Risking Everything: 110 Poems of Love and Revelation* (New York: Harmony Books, 2003), 10.

(Pg 218) **On an episode of *This American Life* called "Superpowers":** The show, "Superpowers," was first broadcast on August 15, 2010 and can be listened to and downloaded here: http://www.thisamericanlife.org/radio-archives/episode/178/superpowers

(Pg 220) **The theologian Ludwig Feuerbach argues in his book:** Ludwig Feuerbach, *The Essence of Christianity,* trans. George Eliot (Amherst: Prometheus Books, 1989), 19–20.

(Pg 220) **We enrich God:** Feuerbach, *The Essence of Christianity,* 73. The full passage in *The Essence of Christianity* reads like this: "The impoverishing of the real world and the enriching of God is one act. Only the poor man has a rich God. God springs out of the feeling of a want; what man is in need of, whether this be a definite and therefore conscious, or an unconscious need—that is God. Thus the disconsolate feeling of a void, or loneliness, needed a God in whom there is a society, a union of beings fervently loving each other."

(Pg 220) **"I am not saying God is nothing":** Feuerbach, *The Essence of Christianity*, xviii. The actual quote from Feuerbach is this: "But I by no means say . . . : God is nothing, the Trinity is nothing, the Word of God is nothing, etc. I only show that they are not that which the illusions of theology make them,—not foreign, but native mysteries, the mysteries of human nature."

(Pg 221) ***We are the ones we have been waiting for:*** June Jordan poem, "Poem for South African Women," quoted by Alice Walker in her book *We Are the Ones We Have Been Waiting For: Inner Light in a Time of Darkness* (New York: New Press, 2006).

(Pg 221) **An Anthropologist's God:** This passage is a combination of direct quotations from Feuerbach's *The Essence of Christianity* and my own words based on my reading of Feuerbach. For more, please see: Feuerbach, *The Essence of Christianity*, 17, 73, 26, 73, 41. I learned that Feuerbach wanted to call the book *Know Thyself* from James C. Livingston's *Modern Christian Thought*. For more, please see: James C. Livingston, *Modern Christian Thought*, vol. I (Upper Saddle River: Prentice Hall, 1988), 223.

(Pg 222) **The Mayan people of Acteal:** I read a version of this story in an article: Anne Llewellyn Barstow, "Violence and Memory: The Politics of Denial, " *Journal of the American Academy of Religion* 68, no. 3 (2000): 591–602.

(Pg 223) **Denis Mukwege, a doctor in eastern Congo:** I read this story in an article published on October 7, 2007 in the *New York Times*, "Rape Epidemic Raises Trauma of Congo War," by Jeffrey Gettleman. The article can be found online: http://www.nytimes.com/2007/10/07/world/africa/07congo.html There is also a slide show on the *New York Times* online called "Sexual Violence in Eastern Congo": http://www.nytimes.com/slideshow/2007/10/06/world/20071002CONGO_index.html

(Pg 224) **In 1977, Carl Sagan was asked by NASA**: I first heard this story on NPR when Eric played the podcast for me. It was originally a RADIOLAB podcast that was picked up by "Story of the Day" on February 12, 2010. You can download it here: http://www.npr.org/templates/story/story.php?storyId=123534818 The

RADIOLAB podcast is called "Space" and can be found here: http://www.radiolab.org/2007/oct/22/.

(Pg 226) **Some people live on top of mountains in glass houses:** Jesse McKinley, "In the Clouds, Sitting Watch Over Paradise," the *New York Times*, October 3, 2007: http://www.nytimes.com/2007/10/03/us/03lookout.html.

ACKNOWLEDGMENTS

Deep gratitude to all who supported me while I wrote this book. Thanks to the readers of many drafts: Mary Adler, Maylen Dominguez, Katie Ford, Brad Monsma, Taura Null, Tovis Page, Eric Toshalis, Amy Walsh. Thanks to the authors of the books I returned to again and again while writing this book: Joan Didion (*The Year of Magical Thinking*), Nick Flynn (*The Ticking Is the Bomb*), Paul Harding (*Tinkers*), Nicole Krauss (*The History of Love*), Sarah Manguso (*The Two Kinds of Decay*), Colum McCann (*Let the Great World Spin*), Jill McCorkle (*Going Away Shoes*). And thanks to the musicians whose songs I listened to on repeat through headphones while writing this book: Reed Foehl, David Gray, PJ Harvey, Gregory Alan Isakov, Ray LaMontagne, Molly Venter. Thanks to the radio shows *This American Life*, *RADIOLAB*, and *Being*. Thanks to Anna Garcia, HanKi Kim, and Juliana Jones. Thanks to Maria Tauber. Thanks to Cesar Aldana. Thanks to my professors

at Harvard Divinity School, especially Karen King and David Lamberth. Thanks to my family—Sentilleses, Toshalises, and Hornbachs. Thanks to 2Lip and Mugu, always asleep on my desk under the lamp. Thanks to my courageous editor, Cynthia DiTiberio, and to all the people at HarperOne who made this book possible, including Amanda Wood, Scott Steinberg, Maria Brock Schulman, and Julie Burton. Thanks to my agent, Elisabeth Weed, friend and brilliant champion. Thanks to Gordon Kaufman—please know this book is a love letter to you, a thank you note. And, finally, thanks to Eric, my love, my home, *hey baby, hey baby, hey.*